Inside
TRACK

INSIDER'S GUIDE TO HORSE RACING

DONNA BARTON BROTHERS
TV COMMENTATOR AND FORMER TOP JOCKEY

LEXINGTON, KENTUCKY

EP
ECLIPSE
PRESS

Library of Congress Control Number: 2011931716

ISBN 978-1-58150-343-2
Printed in the United States
First Edition: 2011

a division of
Blood-Horse Publications
PUBLISHERS SINCE 1916

CONTENTS

INTRODUCTION

My full name is Donna Marie Barton Brothers. I was a jockey from 1987 until 1998 at which time I retired as the second-winningest female rider in the United States by money earned. My mother, Patti Barton, was a jockey. She was one of the first half-dozen women to be licensed as such in the U.S. When she retired in 1984 she was the winningest female jockey of all time. It was not, in fact, until 1988 that her win record was finally broken. You may have noticed I'm very proud of her.

My sister and brother were both jockeys too. My sister married a jockey and retired from competition after becoming pregnant

Riding has been a family affair for the Bartons; from left, Leah, Jerry, Donna, and Patti.

Working for NBC

with their second of four children. She was never really cut out to be a jockey. Just too nice. Not a bad quality, but not a good one for this business. My brother was a *great* jockey but, alas, he took after our father's side of the family and outgrew the occupation by the time he was 18 years old. He started when he was just 16. He's now a horse trainer—Thoroughbreds, of course.

When I retired from race riding I married a Thoroughbred horse trainer, Frank Brothers, and began dabbling in the television side of horse racing. Not long after, I started covering the major races for TVG, ESPN, and then NBC Sports. I currently cover horse racing and a number of equestrian events and disciplines for NBC Sports and cover some horse racing events for TVG.

My early years had me so deeply immersed in horses and horse racing that I was not able to stand back and see that we speak a language unto ourselves in this little world. It wasn't until I started trying to convey racing's stories to a television audience that I realized how far apart the racetrack world can be from the real world. And how *big* the real world is!

Aboard Hennessy, I get nipped at the wire by Unbridled's Song in the 1995 Breeders Cup Juvenile.

With that in mind, I wrote this book to bridge that gap. I'm not sure that I'd ever be able to bring "racetrackers" successfully into the real world, nor do I think they would choose to live there, but I am certain I can bring the casual fan or any other mildly interested party into the world that lies behind the turf and dirt, the silks with sashes, and the beautiful, majestic, and venerable athlete on which this sport is built: the Thoroughbred.

How to use this book

The chapters are organized in order of relevance and your level of curiosity. Each chapter begins with the "basics:" what you need to know on each subject. As you continue to delve into each chapter, I expound on the basics.

If you simply want to know a little bit about every chapter's subject matter read the first two to three pages and then move on to the next chapter. If you wish to know more on any of the subjects, the more you read of the chapter the more knowledge you will glean.

What you can hope to glean from this book

This book will guide you in what to wear to the races and what to take with you. When you're done with the book, you'll have a firm grasp of when and how to bet, what to look for when watching a race, and what to do when you win or (perish the thought) lose.

If you choose to delve further into the subject matter, you'll read about whether or not races are "fixed," why jockeys are so small (and who these little people are), what trainers do, and how owners can afford to buy and race these regal equines.

Next we'll discuss why everyone makes such a fuss over the Kentucky Derby and where these precocious 3-year-old horses compete before and after the big race. I'll clue you in on the best races and race days to attend (outside of the Kentucky Derby, of course), and I'll give you some names to drop (horses and people) so you can sound like you're in the know.

In the final chapter I'll include a list of my favorite racetracks and tell you why they're my favorites. Hopefully, one of them will be near you.

The book also includes quotes from an array of people in Thoroughbred racing who share what they love about the sport.

At the end of this book there's a glossary of terms. You may find yourself using the glossary quite a lot. The racetrack has its own language, and while I try to avoid using esoteric terms, sometimes it is simply unavoidable as these words come up again and again.

I also provide a list of references for books on horse racing as my book covers the basics and you might wish to know a great deal more. This reference guide will help you find what you're looking for.

CHAPTER 1

WHAT TO WEAR TO THE RACES

First of all, have fun with whatever you decide to wear! Below are some guidelines for men and women.

For men: It's easy for you guys. "Jacket and tie required," "No jeans," "No jacket required," etc. They lay it all out for you and all you have to do is know the dress code. The great thing about the track is that if you're in a career that requires you to wear a suit and tie daily you can get away with wearing jeans in most areas. Conversely, if you dress very casually for work and enjoy looking exceptionally dapper from time to time, the track is the place for that too. Bow ties? They're "in" at the track. But so is just about anything else you choose.

(You can now skip to "Here's what you need to know before you decide what you should wear," which you'll find on the next page.)

For women: How many times have you been out shopping for something for work only to spot that fabulous dress? You know the one; we've all seen it—and then we usually follow our great find with the deflating thought, "But I have nowhere to wear it." Well, now you do. That said, what you wear with that great dress depends entirely on two things: where you'll be sitting/standing and what the weather is like, even though neither of these rules is followed at Keeneland in the spring and fall meets by many of the callow but well-intended college students who attend the races.

Keeneland Race Course in Lexington, Kentucky is one of racing's premier locations to "see and be seen." They race two short meets each year: one in the spring and one in the fall and, outside of University of Kentucky basketball games, there's not much else people in that area of Kentucky care about.

Fashion-forward young people soak up the action at Keeneland.

Problem is, these college students, while fashion-forward and proud to attend the races at Keeneland with all of their buddies, plan for this day months in advance. The weather in Kentucky in the spring and fall cannot be predicted days in advance, much less, months. But no matter what the weather is on the day that this momentous occasion finally arrives, they will wear the outfit they picked out so many months ago. Forty-seven degrees, with blowing winds and a 60 percent chance of showers? No matter. You can still bet money that you'll see at least 20 people at Keeneland's legendary racetrack wearing clothing best suited for 80-degree weather. But guess what? They're having fun. And isn't that what it's all about? You, however, will be perfectly coiffed while enjoying the races because you will have done your homework.

Good news for the tomboys too: anything goes at the races. Jeans and T-shirt more your style? That works too.

Here's what you need to know before you decide what you should wear:

Do we have seats?

Where are our seats?

Will we be inside, outside, or both?

If we don't have seats, where do we plan to stand or hang out?

Will we be mostly inside or outside?

How far will we have to walk from the car to the racetrack entrance?

How much walking can we expect to do once there?

Is this simply a sporting event or is it business too?

Whether you plan the trip to the races or you're invited, find out where your seats are and the dress code of that particular section of the track. Even if you don't have the tickets in hand, simply ask the person inviting you where you'll be sitting. It will be written on the tickets. Or pick up the phone—come on, it's not that hard—and call the racetrack and ask the switchboard operator to put you in touch with someone who can advise you about the dress code in your section. Next thing you know, you'll be well on your way

to the perfect outfit. If the person inviting you doesn't already have tickets, chances are they're talking about "grandstand" admission, which I'll discuss in a moment.

Whatever you do, don't forget about the walk from the parking area and back; to and from your seats; and whether you'll be making many trips to the betting windows, paddock, or outside apron or balconies to watch the races live. You'll probably want to wear reasonably comfortable shoes no matter where you plan to view the races. Just make sure they're cute (OK, guys, your shoes don't have to be "cute" but they should be comfortable and not awful).

Best to consider comfort over fashion for a long day at the races on your feet.

Most days at the racetrack require something more comfortable than "door-to-door" (from the car door to the restaurant door) shoes. Besides, jumping up and down while cheering your horse to the finish line and celebrating your winnings with a victory dance for your friends are things best done in comfortable (and safe) shoes.

Finally, remember that a day at the races is usually just that: a day. So in choosing your outfit, keep in mind you'll be wearing it all day. You won't want clothes that are too tight, too loose, or just too uncomfortable to wear all day. Same goes for the shoes.

General guidelines

Racetracks generally have three to four levels of seating and viewing. Grandstand admission is the first and cheapest level and typically does not come with a seat, although you can usually find benches here and there for a brief respite. This is a great way to attend the races if you'd like to keep things on the casual side. But that's not to say the gals can't wear a super-cute dress with flats or that the guys can't throw a sport's coat on with those jeans. Fashion is always, well, fashionable.

Clubhouse admission generally means you'll have a seat somewhere. General clubhouse seating is the second level of admission. The clubhouse usually has a Turf Club which is typically a step above general clubhouse seating. Sometimes clubhouse seats and/or Turf Club seats come with a box outdoors from which to view the races. Also, at some racetracks these boxes can be purchased for the day without dining accommodations.

The highest level of seating at the races comes with an invitation to one of the suites. Generally, the suites are leased by a corporation or a wealthy individual, although the racetrack retains a suite or two to use for its own entertainment purposes. Suites are a relatively new addition to many tracks and not all racetracks have them.

If you're invited to the races by friends, ask them where you'll be sitting, what to wear, and then look forward to the arrival of race day. However, if you are invited either through your own business connections or your spouse's, you should stay on the conservative side of attire—no matter where your seats are located. You can take the party out of the office but you can't take the office out of the party.

Location dictates attire.

Grandstand attire

Check the weather forecast and dress in comfortable clothes and shoes that will be suitable for indoor and outdoor temperatures. Wear the most comfortable pair of shoes you have, as long as they look good.

Your food choices will be of the baseball park variety: hot dogs, hamburgers, pretzels, etc., and you should be prepared to eat standing up. You may be fortunate enough to find a place to sit temporarily while you eat but don't count on it. My advice? Eat before you go and go out to dinner after the races. That is only, of course, if you care about the food you put into your body.

Comfort can be key.

General Clubhouse attire

Typically sports coats and ties are not required for men and jeans are allowed. Shorts are generally not allowed in the clubhouse, but this rule will differ from one track to another so be sure to call ahead and find out. Remember, these are just guidelines.

Clubhouse admission usually comes with a place to sit, often in one of the dining rooms. It's nice because you'll have a table of your own all day and you will have an actual waitress and/or waiter serving you. Plus, you'll still be free to walk around and place a bet, view the horses in the paddock or on the racetrack, or check out the gift shop.

Turf Club attire

Men will likely be required to sport a jacket and tie and women are expected to dress accordingly. Don't forget to bring a sweater or wrap, though, if you decide to wear a sleeveless dress. You'll be sitting in the air-conditioning most of the time.

The food in the Turf Club is usually very good. You may have a menu or buffet to select from and you will definitely have a table to sit at. It's possible that there will be a balcony overlooking the track from where you'll have a wonderful view of the races.

Box seat attire

As mentioned above, oftentimes a box is offered either with your dining room seating or by itself. A box generally seats six and

Dress warmly if you will be spending time outside.

is outdoors. Some are under cover; some are not. Boxes provide great locations from which to watch the races with a group of four to six people and, as they have a railing around them, offer you your own space—and a sort of "safety net" if you over imbibe.

Generally food is not served in the boxes but you may go to one of the concession stands and bring food back to your box to eat. The same applies to beverages.

Obviously, you'll want to dress according to the weather, but you'll also want to observe the rules of the given track. These dress code rules vary widely from track to track.

Private suites attire

You get into one of the suites by invitation only or if you're throwing a big party (typically 10 guests or more) and are able to obtain, for the day, use of one of these private suites. Almost all suites have a private balcony overlooking the racetrack (no safety net here, so be careful). But not all racetracks have suites.

The suites are located in the clubhouse section so you automatically know you have to dress somewhat nicer than you would for the grandstand. How nice you need to dress depends upon who owns the suite, the occasion, and the rules at this particular track. If you receive an invitation to one of the suites simply ask the person inviting you what you should wear.

The food in the suites will vary from one track to another, one suite to another, and one occasion to another. You can expect anything from a buffet of crudités, fruit, and cheeses to a warm buffet or even a sit down meal ordered from a menu.

"Big" day attire

The "big" days are the days that have a marquee race on the card. Each racetrack has at least one big day but how big that day is differs from track to track. Don't be fooled by the word "derby"

> "I was just born horse crazy, which makes no sense because I grew up on the beaches of California surfing, so I think there must be some sort of genetic marker for this. I was just drawn to the sheer beauty and excitement of horse racing and I like the idea that, at least at the highest levels, these horses are doing what they want to do and that they have a good life. And every day I go to the track it confirms that I'm not the only horse-crazy person out there!"
> — *Actress Bo Derek, member of the California Horse Racing Board*

in a racetrack's advertisements for its big day. There's still only one Kentucky Derby and it is, without question or dispute, the biggest of the big days of racing in the United States.

Chapter 10 is dedicated to the Kentucky Derby so I won't delve into that day's attire here. As for the other big days, be sure to ask around. You don't want to overdress or underdress for an important day of racing. What you wear says a lot about you and immediately reveals whether you get what the big day is all about.

Best to dress well if you are invited to a private suite.

So don't be afraid to ask the person who invites you about the attire. If he or she doesn't know (for example, if it's a guy who invites you) then find out where you'll be sitting, with whom you'll be attending the races, and get a phone number for the racetrack. Call and ask them how "big" this day is. Do the women typically wear hats? Do the men wear top hats (they do at some of the European tracks—coat tails too!—but never in the United States)?

Will you be seated in a warm/cool area? Inside or outside? Sit-down dining or simply box seating? Lots of walking or lots of sitting? Are the men expected to wear a coat and tie? Are shorts allowed? You get the idea. Just don't be afraid to ask and don't be intimidated. Before you know it, you'll be an expert on the subject of racetrack attire. Actually, you already are.

WHAT TO TAKE WITH YOU TO THE RACES

Money.

OK, maybe there are a few other items that you should take along too. But money is good. And important. We'll talk more about how much money you should take in the next chapter. For now, let's stick to the basics. Here are the five essential items to take with you:

Money. Yes, it's that important. More in Chapter 3.

Pen or pencil. Trying to decide between your selections in a 12-horse field can be a little bit like taste testing 40 wines at one sitting. Pretty soon they all taste alike. Same with the horses. Pretty soon they all start to look alike. A pen will come in handy

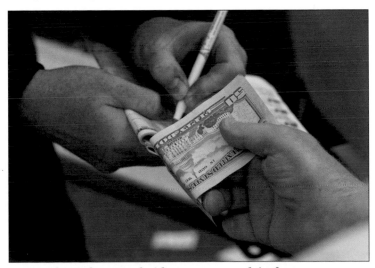

Come to the track prepared with money, pen, and tip sheets.

to jot down notes of what you like or don't like or even to jot down that "hot tip" you get from a friend you bump into who really seems to get this game. Additionally, a pen can come in handy for exchanging phone numbers...You never know.

Tip sheet. Tip sheets are sold at the racetrack if you can't find one before you go. Keep in mind, however, that finding and studying a tip sheet before you go to the races will put you in a better position to impress your friends or colleagues with your wealth of racing information. These tip sheets can be purchased almost anywhere the *Daily Racing Form*[1] is sold. Chances are you'll be able to find a *Form* and a selection of tip sheets at one of the mini markets near the track and you can certainly buy them at the track as well.

Comfortable shoes. I know we covered this in Chapter 1 but it's worth mentioning again. You don't want to be dead weight— or crippled—at the end of the day, do you? And yes, guys, I know I'm wearing you out on this one. But you don't want to be carrying someone to the car, right? Bear with me.

Binoculars. There are at least a hundred TV monitors scattered throughout the racetrack but nothing beats watching a horse race live. Trouble is, it's rather difficult to see what your jockey is doing on your horse unless they are in the final furlong (a furlong is 1/8th

Binoculars will help you focus on the action and impress your friends.

Tip sheets can provide additional insight into betting choices.

of a mile) of the race without a decent set of binoculars. Besides, with these binoculars you'll again put yourself in a position to know more than your friends and colleagues because you'll see more. You'll also enjoy it more. And you'll look like more of an "insider."

Those are the basics. But feel free to bring your lucky coin, rabbit's foot, or a four-leaf clover. These things can't hurt. Aside from that, anything else you might need to bring depends upon where you'll be sitting or hanging out.

If you'll be inside, bring a sweater or wrap. If you're joining a group for a "picnic" day, find out from the racetrack what food and beverages are allowed and bring a cooler with the provisions you'll need.

If you're taking kids, bring some peppermints for them to feed to the ponies. Not the racehorses, the ponies. The ponies accompany the racehorses to the starting gate and, with their riders aboard (these are not jockeys; they're called "pony people" in racetrack lingo), gather near the area where the Thoroughbreds enter and then leave the paddock. They'll wait there while the Thoroughbreds are being saddled in the paddock and, once finished, they'll accompany the racehorses. You need to catch them when the Thoroughbreds are in the paddock. Generally speaking, access to these horses is not too difficult to achieve and most of them appreciate a peppermint or sugar cube.

Also, if you're taking kids, remember their attention spans are short and a day at the races can be long. They'll be thrilled by the horses, jockeys, and racing for about 15 minutes. You might wish to bring a game along to entertain them between races.

When I was a kid attending the races my friends and I would line up in a row on the apron of the track and when the starting gate sprang open and the bell rang we would be off in a herd of unbridled children racing to the finish line along with the horses. Of course, this was at obscure racetracks that had few attendees so the apron was not overcrowded. Attempting this at Keeneland would annoy a lot of people. Another solution? Some racetracks have playgrounds. Very helpful.

What not to take with you to the races

A book or magazine. Not cool. If you want to read between races, read the *Daily Racing Form* and teach yourself more about how to decipher the code of past performances[2]. I learned to read the *Form* when I was 6 years old. It's not hard to read; it's not hard to understand. It's just difficult to learn at first. Once you learn how to read the past performances you'll be miles ahead of most of your friends. Don't be lazy. Just do it. You'll be glad you did. And you'll look super smart.

HOW AND WHEN TO BET

I f you've never been to the races, have not learned to read the *Daily Racing Form*, and did not get a good tip sheet, your best bet is probably not to push very much money through the betting windows. That said, you still need to have a rooting interest in each race or, quite frankly, a day at the races quickly turns into the longest, most boring day of your life.

So, how do you have a real rooting interest without betting a lot of money at the windows? Bet with your friends. If they too are inexperienced, great. If they are experienced players, all the better. There's a reason why they call it "gambling," and even experienced racegoers are just placing money on various levels of educated guesses. But for the never-say-die who are intent on betting their

You don't have to be an expert to place a bet but there is plenty of material to help you make more educated decisions.

Only bet as much as you are willing to lose.

hard-earned dollars with the racetrack I'll give you tips, too. In a minute.

Whatever your betting outlet, the first thing you need to do is decide on a budget. I don't want to bring you down, so hear me out before reacting. "Decide on a budget" is another way of saying, "How much are you willing or can you afford to lose?" You have to remember these beautiful, majestic racetracks with their meticulously landscaped paddocks, infields, and lavish suites were not built on the backs of winners. So be smart about betting. Decide how much you're willing to lose, put only that amount of cash in a pocket or section of your purse designated for wagering, and stick to your guns. And guess what? Before you know it you may have to find another pocket for your winnings as they become so voluminous.

But first things first. Decide how much you're willing to lose for a fun day at the races. Next step, divide that money among a few races. There's a saying among racetrack regulars: "You can beat a race but you can't beat the races." Which simply means you cannot bet every race and win for the day. You can, however, win a race here and there. The trick is to avoid betting the races you have a minimal chance of winning.

Which races do you play; which do you avoid? Stay away from betting very small fields (such as fields with six or fewer horses) unless one of the horses has a really great name and you "just have to" put a couple bucks on it to win. In really small fields there's generally a "stick-out" horse with short odds that will get most of the public's wagering dollars and four or five other horses with more attractive odds but with a much smaller chance of winning. These are what we call "no win" situations. If you bet your money on the heavy favorite, you're risking your cash for very little reward. If you go for one of the longshots you first have to decide which longshot to pick and then reconcile yourself to the reality that the heavy favorite will be very difficult to beat. It's just easier to avoid this kind of race and save your betting money for later.

A note here: When everyone else is deciding who they'll bet on in races with a small field and a heavy favorite, it's a great opportunity for you to take a self-guided tour of the track, visit the gift shop, make a run to the concession stands, or catch up on some text messages you haven't replied to. Also, most racetracks have guides and/or booths in place simply to help newcomers get their bearings. Find one. Now ask all the questions you want.

If you're determined to participate in the wagering action, bet with one of your friends. You can use this strategy throughout the day, and it's a great way to learn more about how to choose a horse and how to watch a race. You both pick one of the longshots and you just bet horse for horse between yourselves. Or, if your friend wants to bet the favorite and you're willing to take a longshot, bet your friend's $10 to your $2. In this bet neither horse has to win for you to win. Your horse just has to beat your friend's horse. You

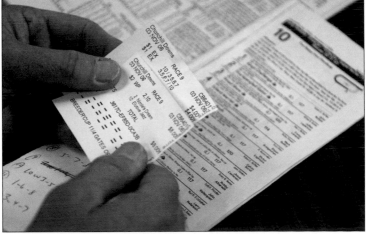

Decide which strategy you'll use when making bets.

> "Both (wife) Barbara and I have always had a fondness for horses, and the beauty they possess. We are very fortunate to have Saratoga Race Course close to where we live. We realized that there are many options when going to the races. You can dress up or dress down and bring coolers and party; the latter was our favorite.
>
> Another factor was the betting aspect and the handicapping needed to figure out the winner. It was really satisfying when you handicap a race correctly and things happen as you planned.
>
> On another note, it is our belief that a day at the races should be a family event and then the experiences are something that can be looked back on as a positive fun memory. We think horse racing racetracks miss this point and should market more towards this happening."
>
> — *Donald Lucarelli, Starlight Racing*

can even bet on who will run last—anything goes here.

For novices peer-to-peer betting is really the best choice and it can be even more fun than winning through the windows. It's definitely more fun than losing through the windows. If you're betting with a fellow beginner you do not need to get too analytical in your handicapping strategy—just bet numbers, jockeys, silks' colors, or names and pit your horse against your friend's horse. Best finish wins, period. You can bet $5, $50, a beer, dinner that night, who-has-to-run-to-the-parking-lot-and-get-the-car, or, my favorite: the victory dance. If you're betting with a date—one with whom you're well acquainted—those bets can get a lot more interesting—and a lot more rewarding. I think you know what I mean. I also recommend buying a drink for whomever you're betting against. It doubles as looking generous so if they're experienced at gambling they may choose to help you in your selections. If they don't help you, keep buying them drinks. Just be sure to drive them home afterwards.

Another way to wager with a group of friends, particularly if one or more in the group is an experienced handicapper, is by pooling funds for a group bet or bets. Everyone in the group should throw in the same amount of money and you should decide in advance if the money will be bet on one race, spread out over a few races, and if you'll use straight win bets, exactas, trifectas, superfectas, etc. (See explanations on next page). If you win, you'll win as a group and nothing is more fun than that. A word of caution: If the group loses every race, things can turn ugly, so if you're the one who suggested starting a group bet, leave for a restroom break around the ninth race and never come back.

Types of wagers

Win: If you bet on a horse to win it has to win in order for you to cash your ticket.

Place: A second-place finish. If you bet on a horse to place your ticket is a winner if that horse runs one or two.

Show: A third-place finish. If you bet on a horse to show your ticket is a winner if that horse runs one, two, or three.

Across the board: Means you are betting on all three positions. A $2 "across-the-board" wager costs $6 and means you've bet the horse to finish first, second, and third. If your horse runs third, only your "show" section of your wager wins. But if your horse wins, you cash for all three positions.

Exacta and exacta box: A "straight" exacta is a bet on two horses in the exact order of finish. For instance, if you bet a 2-7 exacta, the number 2 horse has to win and number 7 horse has to finish second for you to cash your ticket. In an exacta box with the 2-7, either the 2 or the 7 can win and the other one must "place" or run second. You can also add additional horses. Let's say you love the 2 but can't decide among the 4, 5, and 7 for the bottom of your exacta. You can bet a "straight" exacta with the 2 "on top" and the 4, 5, 7 in the second spot. Your 2 horse has to win but in order for you to win, the 4, 5, or 7 can finish second.

Trifecta and trifecta box: Like exacta wagering but with three horses. A "straight" trifecta bet on three horses can only be cashed if your horses run one, two, three in the order in

PAYOUTS ON $2 BET	
ODDS	PAYOUT
1-5	$2.40
2-5	$2.80
1-2	$3.00
3-5	$3.20
4-5	$3.60
1-1	$4.00
6-5	$4.40
7-5	$4.80
3-2	$5.00
8-5	$5.20
9-5	$5.60
2-1	$6.00
5-2	$7.00
3-1	$8.00
7-2	$9.00
4-1	$10.00
9-2	$11.00
5-1	$12.00
6-1	$14.00
7-1	$16.00
8-1	$18.00
9-1	$20.00
10-1	$22.00
15-1	$32.00

which you bet them. If you bet the 2-7-11, they must finish in that order for your ticket to win. The trifecta box allows for your top three selections to run one, two, three in any order and, in addition, you can do a trifecta box with more than three horses. Let's say you also like the 4 and the 5. You can do a 2-4-5-7-11 trifecta box and if any three of those top five selections finish first, second, and third, you win. A word of caution: the more horses you add the more expensive the ticket. A $2 straight trifecta costs just that—$2. A $2 trifecta box costs $24.

Superfecta and superfecta box: Like trifecta wagering but with four horses.

OK, back to the never-say-die group that is intent on betting with the house. Remember step one: decide on a budget. Step two: divide that money up among the number of races you're going to play. Step three: elimination. Look through the program and draw a line through the small field races. You're not playing those races. Now, place one star on the lower-level claiming races, two stars on the upper-level claiming races, three stars on the allowance races, and four stars on the stakes races (if there are any on this card).

Types of races

Your preference for which races to play should go in order of the number of stars: the more stars, the better this race is to play. Stakes-level horses are the most "formful," meaning they run more

Horses in stakes races have more consistent "form."

TYPES OF RACES

TYPE	DESCRIPTION
Stakes Race	The highest level of racing. The horses are the most "formful."
Allowance Race	Between stakes races and upper-level claiming. These horses are not as consistent as stakes horses but they're more consistent than the claimers.
Upper-level Claiming Race	These horses are more formful than lower-level claimers.
Lower-level Claiming Race	The lowest level of racing and the least consistent in performance.

consistently and along the lines of their past performances which you'll find in the *Form*, hence the word "formful." Allowance horses are less consistent than stakes horses but more formful than claiming horses, and higher-level claimers are more formful than lower-level claimers.

At the racetrack a "maiden" is a horse—not the "fair maiden" of your childhood stories—that has never won a race. Maidens can either run for claiming (or, in the lingo of racetrackers, "for a tag," which essentially means they are for sale) or they can run in maiden allowance company. The maiden allowance races are better to play than the maiden claiming races as you can expect to find more highly regarded horses in the latter group.

Now that we know which races we're going to play, it's time to decide which horses we're going to back. As I mentioned earlier, you should try to have some grasp of how to read the *Form* and it doesn't hurt to have a tip sheet with you. Start handicapping each race by first eliminating the three or four horses that would appear to have no chance of winning. Just draw a line through them. Now, for the part that most people totally miss about betting racehorses (and even the experienced bettors miss this part): You're betting on an athlete. When you go to a high school basketball game it's very easy to pick out the true athletes from the want-to-be athletes, right?

And when you watch a professional basketball game it's fairly

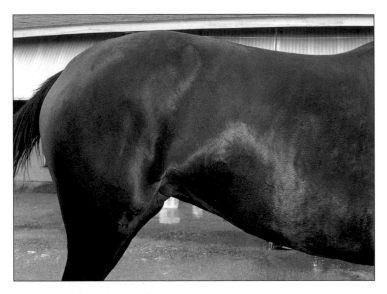

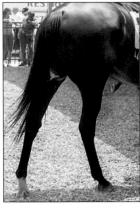

Carrying a little extra weight

easy to tell if a player is fit—or fat. You can tell if the first-season pro, straight out of college, is as toned as the journeymen, right? Well judging horseflesh is much the same. Look for the athlete.

Get out of your chair, go to the paddock, and look at the horses. When a horse is not racing fit the horse is fatter than it should be and it shows in a few areas. The first and most obvious is its belly. Can you see a faint outline of the ribs? Good! You should. Remember, they're athletes. Ribs completely hidden with flesh indicate a "fat" horse that is not fit for this task. What about the hindquarters? Can you identify the two major muscle groups? You should see a clear vertical line that goes down the horse's rump about 4 to 8 inches from the tail on each side. This line should not only be definitive but also fairly long—some 10 to 16 inches depending upon the size of the horse.

"Fat"

It takes a trained eye to tell if a horse is fit, and you'll be able to spot it after you've trained your eye to recognize fitness from the

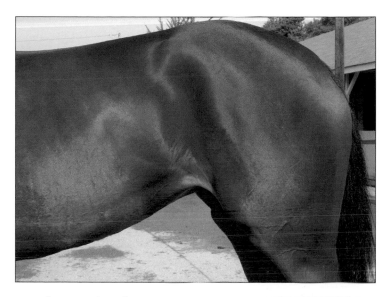

two aforementioned areas.

Look at the horse's flank area. This is the area where the belly meets the hindquarters. Does he or she carry an abundance of flesh in the flank area? A fleshy flank area is not what you want to see. You're looking for a drawn, ready-for-competition athlete.

"Fit"

Some other things to look for: You want your horse's coat (hair) to look

Examples of race-readiness

healthy compared to the other horses. You want to see a nice shine without too much sweat. You do not want to see a dull coat with hair that is sticking up or a horse that has hives (yes, horses do break out in hives and it's almost never a good sign).

You want your horse to look like it has good energy and is excited about what's going on. If the horse is bouncing (we call this "on their toes"), that's good. If the horse is unruly and very difficult to saddle, that's not so good.

You do not want a skinny, puny, or otherwise too-gaunt individual with its head down looking like it dreads what is about to happen. There's a fine line here but you'll start to recognize the

Try to pay close attention to how the horses look before you bet.

signs of a race-ready horse the more you look.

And keep looking. Watch the horses in the paddock. See how they react to having a jockey placed upon their backs; watch them leave the paddock; and then watch them on the track. Even on the track they should be "on their toes" but not jumping out of their skin. They should look excited about what's about to happen—not fearful.

So if you're new to the races don't put pressure on yourself to bet on your opinion right away. Go to the paddock for every race and watch the horses as they go through the saddling procedure. Watch them on the track. Make a note on your program of the horses that just look and act great. Then watch those horses and keep testing your eye until you feel like you've got it. Once you get this down, you're ready to bet. And this is when it's fun to bet against the experienced handicappers because these folks generally pick their horses from the past performances while you'll be picking your horse from the past performances and by what you see in front of you today. And, by the way, aren't they competing today? Now you're ready for some real fun.

It's important to pay attention to the big three: jockey, trainer, and horse. There's a reason why the leading jockeys and leading trainers at a given meet win the most races. Winning begets winning. So if all three of these elements look good on paper and in the paddock then consider betting that horse to win.

How do you know who the top trainers and jockeys are? In the racetrack's program and in the *Daily Racing Form* there will be a "standings" page. The best jockeys win up to 30 percent or more of their races. Coincidence? Don't bet on it. There's a reason why they win so many races and whatever that reason, they're often given the best horses to ride as a reward. Any jockey with a win percentage of more than 20 percent is doing well.

A trainer's job is to condition his or her horses for racing and then find the most suitable spot for each horse to compete. Good trainers know their horses and are good at choosing the best races for their horses' abilities. With trainers, the higher their winning percentage the better.

Betting Do's and Don'ts

Do bet on horses to win: Nobody likes the feeling of betting all day without cashing in on a winning horse. It just isn't good for the psyche.

Don't bet favorites all day: Favorites (the horse in a race with the lowest odds) only win 33 percent of the races so if you bet on them all day, you'll lose 66 percent of the time and the low payout of the winning favorites will not cover your total dollars wagered.

Do be wary if it rains: Muddy tracks compromise horses' performances and horses tend not to run true to form. If you notice a pattern—like horses winning while leading throughout—then try to use that pattern to your advantage by betting on a horse with speed that also has performed well in the past on a wet track.

Do bet exactas—sometimes: If you're really torn between two horses, bet them to run first and second in either order in an "exacta box." Just don't bet exactas every race. It's hard enough to try to pick one horse.

Do bet a dime: Many tracks now have superfecta wagering for 10 cents. A superfecta involves picking the first four finishers in a race so this wager is best left for large fields. You'll have more horses to choose from and the payout will be heftier.

Don't throw your tickets away until you're sure it's a losing ticket and until the race is declared official: If you bet a horse to "show," or come in third, and it wins or runs second, you win. In win, place, and show wagering a "win" ticket only wins if your horse wins, but "place" and "show" tickets are winning tickets if your horse runs better than you expected. For instance, if you bet $2 to show on the 3 and the 3 runs second, you still win. You also win if the 3 wins. The same applies to betting on a horse to place. If it wins, you win.

CHAPTER 4

WATCHING THE RACE: WHAT TO LOOK FOR

The break often determines the outcome of a race. A speed horse (a horse that gets out of the gate quickly and prefers to be on or near the lead in a race) should have a clean break, no bumping into other horses, and no missteps.

A horse that comes from off of the pace[1] should have a good break before dropping back behind the front-runners. Be worried if the jockey is standing up—the horse is probably fighting the rider to do too much too soon and expending too much energy in the process.

The first turn (only applies to route, or two-turn, races): You want a clean run into the first turn. You don't want to see your horse going too fast or too wide, and you don't want to see your

A good break can make all the difference in the outcome.

In a crowded Kentucky Derby, a clean run into the first turn is crucial.

horse's rider having to pull the horse's head up sharply to keep from clipping the heels of a horse or horses crossing in front of him.

The midway point: At this point, you want to watch your horse and the fractions. If you have a speed horse, you don't want it going too fast. ("Fast" is a relative term and differs depending upon the track surface—dirt, mud, slop, or turf—and the distance. More on this subject later in the chapter.) No matter the race, you want to see the jockey on your horse sitting comfortably. If he or she is already "riding" (pushing the horse hard to keep up), that is a bad sign. There's still a long way to go and fatigue will set in for all of them late even if they're strong at this point.

Poles are strategically placed distance markers.

"Pace" refers to the speed of the race as dictated by the front-runners. A solid pace bodes well for a closer and a slow pace helps the front-runners.

The quarter pole (or the "top of the stretch"): On the main track (dirt), 85 percent of eventual winners are no worse than third at the quarter pole (which means there's a quarter mile remaining in the race). You definitely want to see your horse in contention at this point. The exception: On the turf course horses often rally from well off of the early pace and are bunched tightly at this juncture of the race. It's not unusual for the eventual winner to be last at this point.

Turf races can produce close finishes.

Traffic: You don't want your horse to be caught up in too much of it. Much like rush hour, if there's no "lane" open you're not going to be able to pass, even if you're driving the fastest car—or, in this case, riding the fastest horse.

Understanding fractional times

It's not important to understand fractional times to enjoy a day at the races but it will help you understand what's going on better and it will make you look smarter when you share your knowledge with your group.

Before each race starts, check the *Daily Racing Form* or track program to get the track-record time for the race's distance. Your horse probably won't come close to this record but it will give

Fractions for a six-furlong race

you an idea of what it means to be fast or slow. Keep in mind that this record was most likely set on a track termed "fast," not muddy or sloppy. Fractional examples of times to follow are based on a "fast" track. Sloppy and muddy tracks typically produce slower times.

Fractional times are usually posted in the upper left corner of the television monitors and on the tote board in the infield as the race is running. The first time posted will be for the first quarter of a mile; the second time will be for the half-mile fraction; then, depending upon the distance of the race, the times that follow will be for the five-eighths point; three-quarter mile; mile; mile and a sixteenth; etc. You'll see what I mean; just keep reading.

Sprint races: A sprint race is usually competed between a half mile (4 furlongs) and 7½ furlongs. Anything one mile and greater is considered a route race. For this example I'll use the most common sprint distance: three-quarters of a mile or 6 furlongs (remember, each furlong represents an eighth of a mile). In a 6-furlong race, four fractional times will be posted throughout the running of the race: 1/4-mile, 1/2-mile, 5/8-mile, and the final time.

On a fast track in a race going 6 furlongs :22 to :23 seconds

A fast early pace can set up for closers.

for the first quarter is about par; :21 to :21.4 is considered fast. Anything faster than that is considered too fast. Anything slower than :24 is considered a very tepid early quarter. By the way, sometimes racetrackers will refer to the tenth or hundredth of a second as "change," so you may hear that a horse that just posted a :22.3 first quarter mile ran the quarter in "22 and change." Additionally, many tracks now post times in hundredths rather than tenths so you may see :22.65 and hear someone refer to it using the older "tenths" figures as 22 and 3, which it is. But, more precisely, it's :22.65.

The normal time for a half mile is :45 to :46, while anything faster or slower than that range is either too fast to last or too slow for the closers (horses that lay off of the early pacesetters and do their fastest running

> "Growing up in Louisville you can't help but being attracted to the track as a racing fan. For me, it was how captivating the horses were and my heart racing watching them run. (Wife) Laurie and I both shared a passion for horse racing and decided that we'd start a business together around that passion. Favorite aspect? When our horse is faster than anyone else's."
> — *Jack Wolf, Starlight Racing*

at the end of the race) to finish on. That means if you've bet the horse that's on the lead and it just went in :44, it has probably just gone too fast to hang on until the end. That said, if the horse you bet is laying well off of that pacesetter, you're in for a fun stretch run since your horse will have plenty of pace to close on and, hopefully, plenty of energy with which to rally a late charge.

Don't worry too much about the 5/8-mile time. Most people never notice it or discuss it unless it's a 5/8-mile race. So as we skip to the final time, again, refer to your *Form* or program for the track record or recall the times for the day's other races of the same distance. Generally speaking, anything faster than 1:10 (1:07 and change to 1:09 and change) is considered fast. Anything slower than 1:11 and change is considered turtle-like. Unless, of course, the track is slow because of mud or slop or it's just a generally deep and slow track.

Route races: For a mile race you'll see fractions posted for 1/4-mile, 1/2-mile, 5/8-mile, and the mile. If the race is longer than a mile you'll see all of these times posted and then the ensuing ones.

A word of caution here: Some tracks run their one-mile races around two turns and some have a chute along the backstretch of the racing oval that is long enough to accommodate a one-mile race "out of the chute" or around one turn. One-turn mile races will see faster quarter-mile and half-mile times than two-turn mile races because the horses do not have to navigate a turn right out of the gate.

For our purposes, we'll be discussing two-turn mile races and the fractions within. A first quarter mile in :23 and change to :24 is about right. Slower than :24 and the pace is most conducive for the front-runners. By the half-mile point you should see something around a :46 to :49 fractional time. If you bet on a speed horse in a route race and it crossed the half-mile point in :44.3, there's no need to wait for the race to finish to see if you've lost. You did.

In racing one-fifth of a second is considered a length (the length of a horse, about eight feet) and as one full second contains five-fifths of a second, a full second would be considered a five-length margin. So if the fourth race is finished in a time of 1:09.2 and the seventh race is finished in 1:08 at the same distance, you might hear people say that the winner of the seventh race would have beat the winner of the fourth race by seven lengths.

From these examples you should have a pretty good sense of what to look for, time-wise, in the running of the race. Why is this important? So you can at least sound smart if you lose.

CHAPTER 5

After The Race

If you win

Celebrate! But remember, you just beat most of the people at the track, so for good karma's sake use your winnings to buy a loser a drink. And remember, "You can beat a race, but you can't beat the races."

Celebrate a win.

In case of an inquiry

Hold all tickets! Do not throw away or rip up your tickets until the race has been declared "Official." Why? In case of an inquiry. "Inquiries" are posted by the stewards (chief racing officials) and simply mean the stewards are reviewing the running of the race before declaring it official because they have reason to believe that some type of "foul" has taken place.

The stewards have the power to post an inquiry without a jockey or trainer first "claiming a foul," but the jockey and trainer also reserve the right to call the stewards and claim a foul before the race is declared official. You'll notice that in cases of a cleanly run race with no inquiry the race will be declared official even before the jockey gets back, unsaddles his or her horse, and has access to a phone with which to call the stewards.

This is possible because the outriders—always on horseback and in position where the horses and jockeys pull up after the race—are equipped with a walkie-talkie to the stewards. A rider wishing to claim a foul relays the information to the outrider, who in turn notifies the stewards so they can begin the reviewing process even before the jockey returns to unsaddle the horse.

All you need to know, though, is that you should hold your tickets until the race is declared official. The order of finish can quickly change if the stewards believe they've witnessed dirty race riding.

Top 5 excuses if your horse loses

If you lose, feel free to complain as you've bet your money and you've earned that right. Just know what to complain about.

The break: "Did you see how badly my horse got away from the gate?! He didn't stand a chance after getting slaughtered by the 3 horse at the start." If you're going to use this excuse, it helps if your horse actually did get bothered at the gate.

Traffic: "My horse never even got a shot to run! He was jostled around (or blocked) by the other horses the whole way." This is a popular excuse but those around you may scoff at it since, if your horse was really bothered, there probably would have been an inquiry.

The horse: "My horse didn't even try! I mean, did he skip breakfast or what?" This is a good excuse because it takes the blame off of you for picking the horse and places it squarely on the horse.

The jockey: OK, as a former jockey I take personal offense to too much blaming of the jockey, but guess what? That doesn't keep people from doing it. I'm not encouraging here, simply informing. It goes something like this, "Well I guess that's why they call them pinheads! That guy rode my horse like a blind man. She couldn't ride in a boxcar." You get the idea. And I think I've provided you with enough jockey-bashing banter to get you started.

6

ARE HORSE RACES "FIXED"?

I f I had a dollar for every time someone asked me this question I'd be living on the Amalfi Coast of Italy and wouldn't be writing this book because I'd be too busy sunbathing, cruising on my yacht, and ordering my wait staff around. Alas, I'm here—and you're probably wondering about the answer to this oft-asked question.

No, generally speaking, horse races are not fixed. That said, there was a time when many horse races were fixed. But the video camera and television clarity have vastly improved over the years and very little goes undetected with today's technology. Still, even I wonder sometimes about the temptation jockeys and trainers may face to "fix" races at racetracks where the typical purse is around $1,000. It's hard to make a living when the purse doesn't cover the month's training bills.

For now, let's stick with the mid to upper levels of racing you're most likely to experience. At these levels horse racing most assuredly is not fixed. The punishment for fixing races is a lifetime ban from the sport. Lifetime. I cannot stress that enough. It's not like you go to jail for two years then return to your old job at the track. Most people who are involved in horse racing to the extent that they would be in a position to affect the outcome of a race have no life outside of this all-encompassing sport. Racing as a career is more of a lifestyle than a job. A lifetime ban might as well be a death sentence.

Additionally, the purses at the mid to upper levels of racing are so lucrative that winning is enough of a reward. Horse racing may have been fixed when the winning purse couldn't match what a

Stewards, such as Kentucky chief steward John Veitch, watch and review every race.

guy could make through the betting windows. But even back in that era no one person could fix the whole race. In a seven-horse field it would still take the cooperation of at least 10 people—five jockeys and five trainers (assuming that two of the horses simply had no chance of winning anyway). Now if you're thinking that the five jockeys could do it all by themselves, you'd be right; they could. But they still have those five trainers, respectively, to answer to after the race. One "bad ride" could be forgiven but a habit of bad rides will get you fired from those stables and, eventually, you'll run out of horses to ride.

Besides, where jockeys and races are concerned, there are three stewards or racing officials who watch every race very closely. They are always on the lookout for racing fouls (such as crossing into a rival's path) or unusual activity. Riders are fined routinely for not persevering with their mount to the finish line. While this is rarely a sign of "pulling a horse" and is more commonly just a case of the jockey saving the horse's energy for the next race when riding an already soundly defeated horse, the stewards are keenly aware of how bad this can look to the racing public. So unless a horse is unsound or otherwise too weary to cross the finish line, a rider is expected to persevere to the wire in every race. More than a couple of fines for "not persevering to the finish line" will result in a lengthy suspension and, beyond that, will prompt a full-fledged investigation of all of this rider's races, affiliations, etc.

Also, jockeys are not allowed to bet. The only way they can even be associated with a bet is if the trainer or owner of the horse they are riding bets a win ticket for them using their own (the trainer or owner's) money. The trainer cannot bet for the jockey with the jockey's money. Nor can the owner. The trainer or owner cannot bet a "win, place, show" ticket, meaning first, second, or third. They cannot bet an exacta, trifecta, or any other kind of exotic wager for the jockey. They can only bet their own money for the jockey on their own horse and only to win. They can bet any amount of money to win but that's all that they can do.

A jockey will come under immediate and close scrutiny if he or she is even suspected of betting, being associated with betting, "touting," or otherwise being involved with wagering on horses and horse racing. This is not a subject that is taken lightly in the racing world. Again, the penalty for being found guilty of any such activity is, at the very least, a lifetime ban and, at most, a lifetime ban, a huge fine, and jail time.

Now, some people argue that a horse trainer can "stop" a horse back at the barn by giving it some type of medication that will dull the horse and thus its performance, negating the necessity of involving the jockey at all. And while this is certainly true, racehorses are routinely tested for illegal/banned drugs. The one-two finishers of every race are tested—that's *every race*— and a "special" is called in every race. A "special" is a horse the stewards select for drug testing, and it is typically a horse that ran much worse than expected or a horse from a barn that is under suspicion of using banned substances. If neither such horse is present then someone will still be called for a "special." And, of course, every trainer knows this.

The penalty for illegal drug use in horse racing is a hefty fine (usually a minimum of $2,500 for a first offense) and a suspension from racing (usually for at least 15 days for a first offense). A second or third offense brings costlier fines and lengthier suspensions including and/or culminating in a lifetime ban from horse racing.

So, you see, the rules of racing are such to deter and discourage race fixing in any way, shape, or form. I told you earlier that maybe at the lowest levels this could happen but even there, the penalties are the same.

My belief is that even at the lowest level of racing where winning pots are $1,000, by and large racing is on the up and up. An exception may occur when you have someone (or a group of "someones") who is truly desperate to put food on the dinner table or is in jeopardy of losing his or her home. People in such dire straits are certainly vulnerable to the temptation of fixing a race to cash a big ticket. That said, many folks at this level are racing horses as a hobby and have some type of job or business on the side that supports their hobby. They don't find themselves backed into this type of corner because if supporting their hobby becomes too difficult, they can simply sell their horses and get back to their day job. Know what I mean? Besides, "attempting" to fix a race and achieving that goal are two completely different things. It's not easy. And whether you succeed or not, if caught you will be punished severely.

In conclusion, no, I do not believe that Thoroughbred racing (the only form of horse racing with which I am intimately familiar) is fixed. It certainly is not fixed at the highest levels and I would be shocked to learn that it was fixed at any level.

CHAPTER 7

JOCKEYS

D o jockeys talk to each other during races? Yes. They can and do talk to each other during races. But it's not like you might imagine. It's not like trail riding chatter where two or more people ride along talking about the latest news, a good movie they just saw, or what they had for dinner last night (Yes, jockeys eat dinner. Sometimes).

"Talking" is reserved for mostly need-to-know type of stuff, and no, they are not generally chatting with one another as horses load into the starting gate (as depicted in so many horse racing movies). Preparing to ride a race and actually riding a race take tremendous concentration and focus.

Jockeys can be cordial with each other *and* competitive.

The post parade gives a jockey the chance to assess the horse.

First, a jockey prepares to ride by studying the *Daily Racing Form*'s past performances of the horse and its competition. Second, a jockey spends much of the time in the post parade (the warm-up before the race after the horses leave the paddock but before they get to the starting gate) getting to know the horse. This is a very subtle "conversation" that takes place between horse and rider during which a rider can assess how a horse is feeling by the way it carries its head, how and when it moves its ears, how full of or short on energy it is, etc.

Blinkers can keep a horse focused.

A good jockey can learn very quickly if a horse prefers a strong hold on the reins or a very light hold. Hands placed in the middle of a horse's neck versus placing them back near the withers (where the horse's neck meets its back) can induce entirely different reactions in a horse. Some horses are very choosy about where they prefer hands touching them and how much hold they want the rider to have of the reins. In the midst of doing all of this, the jockey is also sizing up the competition—doing all those things I told you about in Chapter 4 because good jockeys know that the past performances tell only part of the story. The rest of the story is prancing around in front of them.

Now horse and rider get to the starting gate, a very small stall that, as you might imagine, is not usually a horse's favorite place to hang out. The break is very important so it's incumbent upon the jockey first to help the horse feel relaxed in the gate and next, to get the horse to stand squarely on all four feet and be ready to break a second before the starter pushes the button that springs the latch on the gates. (The starter is the racing official standing near the starting gate who pushes a button that releases the magnetic field that holds each gate closed. The starter is also the boss of all of the assistant starters—all of those fellows you see leading horses into the gates and then staying in there with some of them.)

So no, there's not a lot of time for idle chatter in the gate. Occasionally, there may be an exchange of need-to-know information such as, "Hey, Mike, my horse was pretty iron-jawed in the post parade and he's wearing a run-out blinker so I wouldn't be surprised if he gets out pretty badly." This would be information conveyed as a courtesy to the rider just to the outside post position of the rider on the horse that looks like he may lug out.

OK, quick definition of all that lingo: "Iron-jawed" means not very sensitive or responsive to the reins. "Run-out blinker" is a blinker[1] that, unlike most blinkers that limit vision equally on both sides, has a full cup only on the outside (or the horse's right side) and no cup on the inside. Because horses are smart and don't like to run where they can't see, the "run-out" blinker is intended to keep them from wanting to bear to the right. And "gets out pretty badly" means a horse that, rather than follow the pack and the inside fence, the shortest way around the track, has a tendency to bear toward the middle or outside of the track, or "lug out."

We've only gotten through the post parade and the gate and already you're worn out, right? Well now we've got a race to ride. But no worries; I won't take you through every step. Suffice to say that if there's that much going on in the stages before the race begins, there's even more going on in the actual race. So yes, there is some talk, but only for information that needs to be conveyed immediately. And yes, sometimes jockeys talk to their horses, but only to help them to relax. "Easy; that's good. Easy." That sort of thing, in a low, comforting tone. The exception is when sweet talk is not working. Then that rider-to-horse chatter sounds more like "You son-of-a-@!^$#..., etc." You get the idea.

Who are these little people and where do they come from?

Jockeys come from all around the world, all backgrounds, all ethnicities, and from both genders. Some are funny, some serious, some work hard, some—not so hard. Some are smart, some have never thought much about anything, some are tall and thin, some are short and stout, but their one common bond is they weigh 115 pounds or less. In fact, it is virtually their only job "requirement." To be a good jockey requires much more than being small enough.

At the highest level of racing all of these people will share another common trait: They are the most amazing athletes you've ever seen. Pound for pound jockeys are the strongest professional athletes of all—bar none. Yes, this includes football players, boxers, wrestlers—you name it. The top jockeys will have them over a barrel when measuring the percentage of muscle mass to their weight and fat ratio. And while most professional athletes maintain fitness by keeping their body fat ratio between 7 percent and 12 percent, jockeys generally have a body fat ratio between 2 percent and 7 percent. Strength is a necessity. But extra weight is not an option.

Imagine if your life revolved around getting on the scale daily and receiving either a "pass" or "fail" grade? Fail to make the weight? You don't get to go to work today. Pass? Great. Now you'll have to get on the scale nine more times. Today. And tomorrow? The same thing. And for every immensely successful jockey there are at least nine others who fight this same battle and risk their lives daily only to make ends meet—at best. Even the very best jockeys still lose 80 percent of the time, so if they don't have a smile on their faces at all times, try to cut them some slack, OK?

But keep in mind: no one makes them do this. They don't have coaches, agents, or parents screaming at them to lose weight.

They are all here because they want to be here and they know that keeping their weight down is part and parcel of riding horses for money at breakneck speeds. They also accept the fact that they will get injured doing this. It's not a matter of if they will get injured; it's how badly, how often, and how quickly they can get back in the saddle.

So why do they do it? Now that's a good question.

"I've been passionate about horse racing since I was 12 years old and began following my older brother Gregg after he became a jockey. I fell in love with the sport because of its excitement, beauty, and splendor. I have remained passionate about it because these wonderful equine athletes teach us something new each and every day. I cannot think of a more interesting or exciting way to make a living than working with thoroughbred racehorses.."
— *Retired jockey Chris McCarron, founder, North American Racing Academy*

Jockeys are a confluence of many traits, temperaments, attitudes, backgrounds, and manners. They generally come from one of two places: Either they grew up in the horse racing business and hoped they would stay small enough to be a jockey or they were just very athletic individuals who did not grow as much as their teammates or playmates, and somewhere along the line someone suggested they should be a jockey.

Like most great athletes, jockeys were generally athletically gifted from a young age. And in most states the legal age requirement for a jockey is just 16. But unlike high school and college athletic standouts, a young rider has no requirements with regard to grade point averages, curfews, or behavior "off the field." And success attained before emotional and mental maturity are gained can be dangerous. Many of these young men meet with success early and gain admiration for none of the really important characteristics that turn a young man into a gentleman.

The lucky few have parents looking over their shoulder at every turn, helping them save their money and not get caught up with the wrong crowd. They are the lucky few. The others? Well, if they survive their apprentice year[2] without causing too much disruption in their own lives and the lives of those around them, they are well on their way to becoming successful at something very few people will ever be lucky enough to try. These are proud men with something to prove, riding tall in the saddle, whip in hand, feeling more at ease on the back of a horse than anywhere else in the world.

And while it's true there are also many female jockeys, I don't mention them in the above description because male and female jockeys generally differ vastly in how they arrive at the same occupation. Male jockeys are often strong-willed, athletic competitors whose friends and classmates all grew bigger than them. So they find themselves fighting a "little man's ego" and working hard to prove their worth in a world of much taller people. They did not grow into the sports they were good at when they were young. Baseball? No. Football? Not so much. Basketball? Fugettaboutit! And so they almost inevitably go through a rough patch finding how and where they fit in.

The girls? Well, let's face it; being 5' 2" and 100 pounds is great—if you're a girl. And most women enter this profession because they were first attracted to the horse and, along that line, horse racing, and stayed small enough to do it. But often they too wage the same war against weight gain while having to work harder than their male counterparts (thanks to baby-making genetics) to build the necessary muscle mass required to do this job well.

Why do jockeys have to be so small?

A question I hear often. Simply because of the strain that the high speed of racing while carrying a saddle and rider puts on the spindly legs of the massive yet athletic Thoroughbred. There have been many arguments for and against raising the scale of weights. The bottom line is, the scale of weights must remain on the low to lowest possible end to protect the soundness of the Thoroughbred. And the truth is, there's no shortage of small people wishing to don white pants and compete in horse races. Just as having a great throwing arm is a prerequisite for a quarterback, so is weighing in at under 115 pounds a necessity for a jockey.

At the end of the day, there are so many remarkable stories about jockeys—both male and female—and where they came from and how they arrived at this occupation that it is not only beyond the scope of this book but excellent fodder for a future book. For now, please refer to the books on this subject listed in the references. They are all very good. And these jockeys are worth getting to know better. For us, it's time to move on to horse trainers.

8

TRAINERS: HOW DO YOU "TRAIN" A HORSE?

I n Thoroughbred racing we work with only one breed of horse: the Thoroughbred. Why is this important to know? Because it helps to know that each breed of horse has been bred over many centuries to specialize in a particular discipline. Thoroughbreds have been bred for hundreds of years to do one thing: race. But it is the Thoroughbred trainer's job to get them physically fit for racing while keeping their mind from getting, well ... too racy.

By the time a horse makes it to the racetrack, it already knows how to lead, carry a rider, jog and gallop, enter a starting gate, and stretch its stride to near-race speed.

Early lessons in leading take place on the farm where the horse is raised. By the end of its first year, a horse usually goes to a breaking facility where it gets a rider on its back and learns its early lessons. Doesn't sound like there's much left to "train" them to do, right? Not so.

Once a Thoroughbred makes it to the racetrack the trainer's job is to assess the horse's status and move it toward its first race. The horse will come with some notes from the breaking facility about its tendencies and/or idiosyncrasies. The breaking facility will let the trainer know if the horse has ever moved faster than a gallop and how fast and far it has gone.

The trainer's job is not only to get this young, generally unfit horse to its first race and beyond but also to the most suitable race. The trainer has a lot of help in doing this. He or she has grooms who care for the horses, exercise riders who ride them, "hotwalkers" who walk the horses to cool them out after exercising, farriers

Some trainers accompany their horses to the track in the mornings.

who shoe them, veterinarians who care for them, and yes, even horse dentists to work on their teeth. But it is the horse trainer's job to assign the groom, hotwalker, exercise rider, and jockey to each horse. And then all of these individuals receive instructions from the trainer about what to do with each horse each day.

It's also the trainer's job to decide which race to run a horse in. This is easier said than done. The trainer has to decide: Will this horse do best sprinting or running a longer distance? Will the horse prefer racing on the dirt or grass? The trainer determines much of this by watching the horse and how it moves but also through trial and error.

Pedigree also plays an important role. Great turf horses (horses that excel at racing on the grass course) go on to produce offspring that often show an affinity for the turf too.

This entire process is much harder than it sounds. The hardest thing to do when it comes to training is to get a horse fit enough to run the first time. If the trainer pushes the horse too much too soon it can come up with minor injuries that will force the trainer to back off. Sometimes these injuries happen anyway, but pushing a horse too early will surely cause them. And ignoring minor injuries almost assuredly leads to major injuries.

It's just like with people: getting fit is a lot harder than staying fit. But the fine line a horse trainer must maintain while getting a Thoroughbred fit doesn't just involve keeping it sound but also preventing the horse from getting too wound up mentally. The physical fitness and mental preparedness must come together at precisely the same moment. Otherwise, it's like dealing with a Jack Russell puppy that never gets to go out and play—it just sort of destroys things.

To understand this whole process a little better let me back up some. To begin with, there is a "breeding season" in the Thoroughbred industry that runs from around the second week of February through the first week or so of July. The gestation period for a Thoroughbred is 11 months, so the breeding season is designed to deliver foals sometime between January 1 and June 1. To keep matters relatively simple in this business, all Thoroughbreds turn one year older on January 1 regardless of their exact birth date. This makes foaling as close as possible—but not before—January 1 ideal.

A baby horse is called a foal until it is weaned from its mother at about six months of age. It then becomes a "weanling" until it turns 1 on January 1. They are then called "yearlings" until they turn 2. Once horses are weaned they spend the next year or so running the fields with their generation of playmates. This is their childhood, so to speak.

Young horses enjoy childhood play before training starts.

Training has many facets.

In the late fall of their yearling year they are generally broke to ride. Some horses are broke to ride at the farm where they are raised but most go to a breaking facility that specializes in this stage of development. They will spend the next several months learning early lessons under saddle.

In the spring of their 2-year-old year, if they are precocious and exhibiting all the signs of being ready to race, they will be sent to the racetrack to begin their racing careers. Some go to 2-year-olds in training sales.

Many horses are not ready to race at 2—at least not early in the year. Some just don't display the speed required to race at this stage when the races are all sprints and the ones quickest away from the gate usually win. Some develop little injuries that indicate too much is being asked of them. But by the time a horse actually makes it to the track, it has a solid foundation through months of preparation.

Back to the trainers—you now know what they do and have a little bit of an idea about how they do it. But who are they?

Not unlike jockeys, many horse trainers are sort of born into the industry. Two of the country's leading trainers are Steve Asmussen and Todd Pletcher. Steve's father was a jockey; his mother was a horse trainer. His only brother was a jockey. All of his family is still involved in the industry. Todd's father, J.J. Pletcher, was a horse trainer and now owns and operates a large and beautiful horse breaking facility in Ocala, Florida. Before turning to the same profession Todd went to college, even though it was anticipated he would become a trainer.

That said, a large portion of trainers are just people who always liked horses, rode them at some point, and then later decided to try to make a living out of doing what they love. My husband, former horse trainer Frank L. Brothers, is a perfect example of this second group. He grew up in New Orleans, Louisiana, and rode horses as a young boy and teenager. He tried college for a while, but when I asked him what courses he took he quickly replied, "Time and space." As he put it, he was anxious to get back to working with horses and always believed he could make a living with them.

Like many successful horse trainers today, Frank got his start by walking "hots" at his home track, Fair Grounds Race Course, where he asked the leading trainer there, Jack Van Berg, for a job. He started at the very bottom (as a hotwalker) and worked his way up the ranks (groom, shedrow foreman, exercise rider) to assistant trainer. He worked for Van Berg for 10 years before starting his own stable in 1980. His story is like so many others.

Whatever one's background, getting started as a trainer takes both a solid foundation steeped in working with horses and a fairly hefty financial commitment. To address the first issue, in order for a trainer to receive a license he or she must pass a test issued by the state's racing commission. The test will assess the would-be trainer's ability to understand and cope with both basic injuries to a horse and complicated injuries. They'll need to know everything from how to apply bandages to a horse's legs to how to enter a horse in the right race.

On the financial end, they'll need to have enough capital to buy the stable's equipment: stall webbings, feed tubs, water buckets, horse blankets, bandages, brushes, foot picks, pitch forks and rakes, muck bins and wheelbarrows, saddles, saddle cloths, saddle pads, bridles for training and racing, halters and shanks, wall boxes and foot boxes (to store equipment), medicines, liniments, etc. The list goes on and on, especially when you're paying for it.

In addition to finding horses to train, they'll also need to find employees. So they'll need to have enough start-up money to pay hotwalkers, grooms, exercise riders, etc. And they'll need to obtain and pay for worker's compensation insurance and some type of limited liability insurance. Given the financial commitment and the time it takes to learn the skill set to train Thoroughbred horses you have to wonder why anyone would ever choose this occupation. It all comes down to the love of the horse. And a guy or a gal believing they'd be miserable trying to earn a living doing anything that didn't involve working with these magnificent and mysterious creatures.

As you may imagine from the information you've gleaned so far, training a horse, though not without its challenges, is the easiest thing a good horse trainer does. Other challenging aspects include dealing with inevitable injuries and trying to minimize them as much as possible, managing employees, communicating with the owners of the horses, building relationships with jockeys and finding ones who can easily adapt to each horse's particular quirks and running styles, and dealing with jockey agents, the starting gate crew, the racing secretary, etc. It really never ends.

But while training a horse well is the most important thing a horse trainer can do, the second most important asset is to be a good communicator, especially to communicate well with the horse's owners. That's because even the most fervid horse lover cannot train horses without the owners. The owners buy the horses and pay the bills, in turn allowing the trainer to pay his or her own bills.

9

OWNERS: WHERE DO THEY COME FROM?

Horse owners come from all walks of life and many are very wealthy. A hefty bank account is not required for horse ownership but it sure helps. The expenses involved with owning racehorses can be astronomical. That said, there are some wonderful syndicates that sell interests in horses, allowing the Average Joe to get involved in horse racing on levels that were previously cost prohibitive.

In the preceding chapter we discussed the developmental stages of the Thoroughbred. What we failed to mention is that someone is paying bills on these horses every day of every stage. Even before the horse is conceived someone paid for the stallion's fee. The stallion fee (also called a stud fee) can range from $500 to a recent-year high of $500,000. Then, as mentioned earlier, the gestation period is 11 months. So someone has to pay for the mare's boarding and care during this time. It's not uncommon for a quarter of a million dollars or more to be spent on a Thoroughbred foal before it even hits the ground.

That "someone" paying the bills is the horse owner, and as soon as the foal hits the ground the owner is paying a boarding fee on two horses rather than one. If the breeder is the farm owner, he or she will be paying to feed two once the foal is weaned. You think children are expensive to feed? Try having a 500-pound "child." Plus, there are the auxiliary expenses of vet care and horse shoeing. Yes, horse "shoeing." Even though they are not wearing horseshoes at this stage, their feet still need to be trimmed regularly.

A horse that makes it to the races by age 2 has already generated about $50,000 in bills, not including the stud fee. And training at the track is even more costly—an estimated $40,000 to $50,000 a year in training, veterinarian, and farrier bills. You can see why it's been coined "The Sport of Kings." It takes a king's ransom to pay for one horse.

By now you have to be wondering why anyone in his or her right mind would ever get involved in this. I think many horse owners ask themselves that same question daily. But when pressed for an explanation they all report that the thrill of having one of their horses win a race—no matter how small or large the purse—makes it all worthwhile. Of course, they all dream of getting that one really, really good horse.

Owners dream of getting the really good horse.

Horse owners are often as disarmed by the love and affection they have for their horses as they are by the love they feel for their own children. The time and expense required to get a horse to the races allow an owner to develop a real understanding of the horse, if not a real relationship with it. And, as many of you know already, horses have unique personalities, making getting to know them rewarding.

Plus, as many horse owners point out, it's a "hobby" they can share with family and friends. Yes, the owner pays all the bills. But many hobbies are expensive. Boating, skiing, vacationing, etc., are expensive hobbies but at least in horse racing you get the chance to win. And although the owner alone pays the bills, family and friends always share the win. The only thing better than winning is sharing that win with people you love. Going to the races for the day can be a fun way to share time with family and friends, and having your own horse running that day makes it even more exciting.

Aside from the love of the horse and the desire to own a really fast one, horse owners have little else in common. They come from all walks of life, have succeeded in all varieties of businesses, and have as many different personalities as there are beautiful flowers in the world. But the racetrack is one of the few places in the world where you'll see a billionaire businessman talking at length with a minimum-wage worker born in Ecuador about something they both care about. Both of these people have a horse that belongs to them: the worker, or groom, cares for it and thinks of it as one of his children, and the billionaire owns it and thinks of it as one of his children. They both love it, which gives them common ground. And something to talk about.

There are just too many interesting owners and stories to tell to get into them here.

I'd be remiss not to add a note about breeders here. In the program or *Daily Racing Form* you'll see the names of the horse, jockey, trainer, owner, and breeder.

> "I was obviously raised on Claiborne, but I don't think that is why I was drawn to the business. From an early age I loved the animal and riding. When (homebred champion) Moccasin was a 2 year old, I really started to love the racing end of it. Being part of a good horse will make anyone love racing. The best thing is you can bet on a horse and suddenly he is your horse—no other investment than two dollars. I continue to love racing as it is one of the most beautiful as well as challenging sports. Nothing is more exciting than to watch a 2 year old breezing hoping he might be the next one. Or how about (homebred champion) Blame before the Breeder's Cup as he got ready for a war? And the handicapping is so challenging with all the factors to put into 'your horse.' And on top of all that—the social aspect."
> — *Claiborne Farm's Dell Hancock, a fourth-generation owner/breeder*

Sometimes the owner and breeder are one and the same, meaning the person who owns the horse also bred it. This means they owned the mare that produced the horse you see in the program.

Oftentimes, horse breeders try to stay out of the racing game. They produce Thoroughbreds based on their knowledge of the breed and then endeavor to sell the offspring for a profit at auction. Some breeders sell everything, with no reserve, meaning they set no minimum on the amount of money they'll take for their horse at auction. Most set what they consider a fair reserve and will keep the horse to race if it doesn't bring the anticipated price.

Some horse breeders are also horse owners and their goal is to produce the best horses possible, race the ones they believe have a chance of success, and sell those they think will be subpar. Of course, this is a lot like looking into a crystal ball and they are not always right, sometimes keeping the slow ones and inadvertently selling the fast ones.

The last group of owner/breeder is the owner who has no intentions of turning into a breeder. These owners just want to race horses and ideally sell those horses at the end of their careers to people who want to breed. But, as often happens, an owner falls in love with a horse and simply cannot bring himself to part with it even when its racing days are over. These owners unwittingly enter into the breeding game, sometimes with great success, sometimes at a great financial loss. Such is the game. But at the back of everyone's mind, owner and breeder alike, is one race. The one race everyone wants to win more than any other. Turn the page...

THE KENTUCKY DERBY
WHY SO MUCH FUSS OVER THIS ONE RACE?

I rvin S. Cobb (1876-1944), a verbose journalist and accomplished author originally from Paducah, Kentucky, was asked to explain the emotion the Derby evoked in Americans. "If I could do that," he said, "I'd have a larynx of spun silver and the tongue of an anointed angel. Until you go to Kentucky and with your own eyes behold the Derby, you ain't been nowheres and you ain't never seen nothin'!'"[1]

Not having more adequate words to describe why you just have to be there I'll thank him (posthumously) for allowing me to use his words to introduce the subject.

The Kentucky Derby. It is glitz and glamour mixed with the most basic and pure love of an animal and the thrill of competition. It combines the most amazing athletes, both human and equine,

The Kentucky Derby is a uniquely American sporting event.

competing for the sport's most coveted prize, with everyone from self-proclaimed rednecks to the Queen of England in attendance. There is, quite simply, something for everyone. The Kentucky Derby is no longer a race; it's an event. If you just love a great party, come to the Derby. If you just love horses, come to the Derby. If you care nothing about either of these things and are only drawn to the best gambling opportunities, come to the Derby. If you want to hang out with your friends or if you have no friends, come to the Derby. You just have to see it to truly get it.

The first running of the Kentucky Derby took place on May 17, 1875 and was contested around the same oval where it's run today. The Derby is the longest-held, continuously contested sporting event in the United States and was a hit from its inception. The event consistently draws crowds upwards of 130,000 people with the record of 164,858 set in 2011. The previous record had been established in 1974, the Derby's 100th anniversary. Just imagine the energy in a stadium filled with 20,000 people watching a basketball game or a football game. Now multiply that by seven and let everyone walk around with a drink in hand. Oh, and add betting windows.

And the thing about the Derby is that it only lasts for two minutes, so it's really all about the party. The great thing is, you can come early and stay late or come late and leave early but to really get the essence of the main point, the race, you only have to pay attention for two minutes. The rest of the time you can have lunch, hang with your friends, bet on other races, or just watch people. You've never seen so many fabulously clad individuals on one day in your life and you've never experienced such collective anticipation. Guaranteed.

If you're paying attention you'll notice you've just read an entire page about what makes the Derby so spectacular and I've barely even mentioned the horses. Truth be told, you really don't need to know a thing about horses or horse racing to enjoy the Kentucky Derby experience. But it does help, and will only enhance your experience.

The Kentucky Derby is the race everyone in horse racing wants to win, and having won it already only whets the appetite to win it again. And not just because it carries with it a $2 million purse. From the time a young horse comes to the track, particularly if it is a boy horse that shows any talent at all, everyone around it covertly thinks, "Derby?"

That said, just wanting to win the Kentucky Derby will not get your horse in the race. The horse has to earn his or her way there and I'll talk more about that later. For now suffice to say that on the first Saturday in May[2] when the Derby field is loaded into the starting gate and just before the latch springs open, you are looking at the largest gathering of the most talented 3-year-old horses that have been sound and healthy enough to get to this point. Not only is it the best race you've seen all year up to this point, it's the toughest race any of these horses has ever run in. It's the very best facing the very best.

> "I love the satisfaction of showing and racing a good horse, whether I've ridden them or trained them. Horses are amazing animals to work with and the good ones are good in spite of their rider or trainer. When you know you've done it right there's an enormous feeling of accomplishment."
> — Michael Matz, silver-medal-winning Olympic show jumper and Kentucky Derby-winning trainer

Winning this race can make careers. Winners that are colts will get an instant leg up as a future stallion. For the winning jockey, trainer, owner, and breeder, victory in the Derby can be so much more than a feather in their cap. It can be the crowning achievement to an already great career or the catalyst to one. There is no single race in America that holds more meaning, significance, and implications than this race. So...that's why all the fuss over this one race.

A note for clarification: any thoroughbred race called a "derby" is for 3 year olds only. Any Thoroughbred race called an "oaks" is restricted to 3-year-old fillies. Boys are not allowed into races restricted to girls but the "boys" races are considered "open" races, and thus girls can race with them if their connections choose to do so. On a related subject, "futurities" are for 2 year olds only and "handicap" races are for older horses (3 and up).

What to wear

As with any other race day, what you wear should depend upon where you are seated or what section you'll be hanging out in. While a beautifully fitted dress looks amazing with the perfect custom-made hat, neither of these articles of attire will look appropriate in the infield. Same goes for the guys: a white suit? Perfect for the clubhouse. For the infield? Big mistake. Conversely, infield attire will leave you feeling poorly dressed should you venture to the clubhouse.

Here's an insider's tip for the ladies: First course of action is to find out where you'll be watching the day's races from. Second? Buy two outfits. Yep, you read that right. You'll return the one you didn't wear after the Derby but it's impossible to know exactly what the weather will be like on Derby day a month or even a week out when you'll most likely be doing your Derby attire shopping. Buy an outfit that will be ideal for a beautiful and warm sunny day and buy another outfit that will be stylishly warm should cooler weather prevail. That is the biggest secret of women who show up every year at the Derby in the perfect outfit. In a perfect world these two outfits would be along the same color scheme so you only have to buy one hat, but let's be honest—it's hard enough to find a hat to match one outfit, not to mention two. So good luck with that.

For the men? One outfit will work. If it's colder than you hoped you can always add a sweater under your suit or sport's coat and wear a T-shirt too. Of course, you knew that already. Something you may not know: if you like bow ties the Kentucky Derby is actually the ideal spot for such fun and unique sporting attire. It's sort of a throwback to classic fashions for men and with the Derby's long history and flair for fun, what better place to pull out the bow tie? Other than that, men's attire is easy—as usual.

Churchill Downs on Kentucky Derby day has all of the same seating and viewing areas mentioned in Chapter 1 but on that day the track uses the infield (on Kentucky Oaks day too, the day before the Derby). So refer back to Chapter 1 for appropriate attire guidelines and then plan to step it up a notch for Derby or Oaks day. Infield attire? Anything goes! Just don't overdress and it's virtually impossible to underdress unless you wear your birthday suit. If you're unsure about what kind of hat and/or dress to wear, visit the Kentucky Derby website. There are lots of photos of fashionably clad men and women from Derbies past and you can get some ideas about what might work for you.

Beautiful hats are a Derby tradition.

But anything goes.

Oh, and umbrellas are not allowed at the track as they obstruct the view of those behind the umbrellas. So while you're shopping, make sure you pick up a suitable raincoat or even a $2 plastic poncho in case of rain.

Whatever your clothing, make sure it's comfortable. A day at the races is all day and on Derby Day there's even more spacing between the races so it's a longer day with more people than on any other race day. In fact, I generally recommend that people either arrive early and leave early or arrive late and leave late. Getting there for the first race and staying through the Kentucky Derby is too long of a day for many people to enjoy thoroughly. And I really want you to enjoy your Derby experience.

On a related note, if you're planning to go out to eat dinner after the Derby make sure to secure your dining reservations well in advance of the first Saturday in May. Also, give yourself time to freshen up between the races and dinner if possible, especially if you've been at the track all day. This may mean planning to dine at a restaurant whose location will allow to stop by your house or hotel first. You'll be grateful for a chance to freshen up before dinner and maybe even change clothes and, if you're wearing a hat all day, you'll probably want to get out of it and take a moment to address that "hat hair" problem.

With this in mind, give yourself time to hit Derby traffic when leaving the track and then squeeze in that quick touch up. If you plan to stay for the Big Race—and you should—don't even think about making a dinner reservation until two hours after the race is run.

Kentucky Derby "prep" races you need to watch

Truth be told, you don't need to watch any of the preparatory ("prep") races leading up to the Kentucky Derby to enjoy the Derby but it will definitely enhance your Derby experience and make you sound way smarter than those who have not watched them. Plus, graded stakes earnings determine the field for the Kentucky Derby[3] and trainers use these prep races to earn enough money for their horse to make the cut. A note here: I'll say "the Derby" quite a lot and, in fact, there is more than one "derby." But anytime someone in America says "the Derby," they mean the Kentucky Derby.

The most important prep races, in both readying a horse for the Kentucky Derby and in determining who the favorites will be, take place three to six weeks in advance. However, unlike the Kentucky Derby which is always run on the first Saturday in May, some of the preparatory races move their dates up or back a week at times. As of this writing the first major prep is six weeks out and it's the Louisiana Derby at the Fair Grounds in New Orleans. Also on that day there's a prep at Turfway Park in Florence, Kentucky. It's currently called the Vinery Racing Spiral Stakes (but its name has changed many times). Five weeks out you'll want to watch the Florida Derby run at Gulfstream Park in Hallandale Beach, Florida, and the Wood Memorial Stakes contested at Aqueduct Race Track in Jamaica, New York.

Four weeks before the Kentucky Derby tune in to the Santa Anita Derby from Arcadia, California, and three weeks out you'll need to watch the Blue Grass Stakes run at Keeneland in Lexington, Kentucky, and the Arkansas Derby from, you guessed it, Arkansas. Hot Springs, Arkansas to be more precise.

You'll notice these prep races are run all over the United States and that's really what makes the Kentucky Derby so engrossing. Regional stars begin to emerge from these preps and you'll end up with an undefeated horse from California, a lightly raced but precocious star from Florida, a tried and true runner from Arkansas, and similar standouts from New York, Louisiana, and Illinois all facing each other for the first time when they line up in the starting gate for the Kentucky Derby.

And those are just the prep races you need to watch. In covering the Kentucky Derby I begin watching horses, with a keen eye toward the Derby, in the summer and fall of their 2-year-old year. Only one horse (Big Brown in 1998) has ever won the Kentucky Derby without having raced at 2, and there's a good reason for this. The horse that wins the Kentucky Derby needs to combine precocity, talent, and soundness. Horses that do not race at 2 typically don't make it to the races at that age because they're either slow to develop (mentally and/or physically) or have had setbacks from injuries. A "soft-boned" horse will not survive the Derby Trail and stay sound enough to compete in the Derby.

The horse that wins the Breeders' Cup Juvenile Stakes in the fall of its 2-year-old year is typically the tepid favorite for the Kentucky Derby to be run six months later. First of all, this horse has to be good to win the race as it's generally a full field of 14 and secondly, he earns enough grades stakes money on that day to ensure a berth in the Kentucky Derby.

Most of the good horses that have proven themselves at 2 get some time off in the winter and won't generally race in December and January. I'm painting with a very broad brush here so there will be many exceptions to this traditional pattern. The Kentucky Derby "preps" really begin in about February of their 3-year-old year. Below is a list of the most significant ones in order of the dates that they are run as of this printing.

FEBRUARY

Robert B. Lewis Stakes *at Santa Anita Park in Southern California*

Whirlaway Stakes *at Aqueduct in New York*

Sam Davis Stakes *at Tampa Bay Downs in Florida*

San Vicente Stakes *at Santa Anita Park*

Southwest Stakes *at Oaklawn Park in Arkansas*
Fountain of Youth Stakes *at Gulfstream Park in South Florida*
Hutcheson Stakes *at Gulfstream Park*
Risen Star Stakes *at the Fair Grounds in New Orleans,*
Louisiana
El Camino Real Derby *at Golden Gate in Northern California*

MARCH

Gotham Stakes *at Aqueduct*
San Felipe Stakes *at Santa Anita*
Rebel Stakes *at Oaklawn Park*
Tampa Bay Derby *at Tampa Bay Downs*
Swale Stakes *at Gulfstream Park*
Louisiana Derby *at the Fair Grounds*
Vinery Racing Spiral Stakes *at Turfway Park in Florence,*
Kentucky
UAE Derby *at Meydan in Dubai*
Sunland Park Derby *at Sunland Park in Sunland Park,*
New Mexico

APRIL

Florida Derby *at Gulfstream Park*
Santa Anita Derby *at Santa Anita*
Wood Memorial Stakes *at Aqueduct*
Illinois Derby *at Hawthorne Race Course near Chicago, Illinois*
Arkansas Derby *at Oaklawn Park*
Blue Grass Stakes *at Keeneland in Lexington, Kentucky*
Coolmore Lexington Stakes *at Keeneland*
Derby Trial* *at Churchill Downs in Louisville, Kentucky*

*The "Derby Trial" is a bit of a misnomer. First, it's not a "trial" for the Derby and it's run just one week before the Kentucky Derby. Second, technically speaking, it is a prep race for the Kentucky Derby, but no one has used it as such in many years. It's just too close to the Kentucky Derby and there are many more suitable options from which to choose.

As for how to watch all of these races, well if you live in an area where you get one of the horse racing networks with your basic cable package it's fairly easy. If not, you may have to visit a racetrack that has simulcast wagering and thus shows races from all over the United States (and beyond) or go to the racetrack's website and watch them there. You can also just read about them in the sport's section of your local newspaper or go to the *Daily Racing Form*'s website (www.drf.com) or the *Blood-Horse* magazine's website (www.bloodhorse.com). Some of the preps will be shown on network television as well but which preps and which network will carry them changes almost annually.

Whether you're lucky enough to go to the Derby or just watch it from someone's Kentucky Derby party or your own party, being familiar with these prep races will not only make you look smarter they'll help you to bet smarter.

That said, I always recommend betting the Derby only for fun. In other words, don't bet more money than you can comfortably afford to lose. The Derby is a notoriously tough race to win both for a horse and for a bettor. This is the first time any of these horses has raced in a 20-horse field and they are facing the stiffest competition to date and the largest and most uproarious crowd they'll ever encounter. Getting good position going into the first turn is paramount to a good performance and everyone is vying for that same "good position." So do your homework. Know who to watch and why. Now sit back and enjoy the best race of the year.

Where do Derby horses go after the Derby?

Good question. Actually, I think I just patted myself on the back. In any case, while the Kentucky Derby is the biggest race we have it's only the most important race we have until it's been run that year. After the Derby has been contested there are many more significant races in which to compete, including the Preakness Stakes and the Belmont Stakes, the two remaining legs of the Triple Crown.

As I said before, the Kentucky Derby is always contested on the first Saturday in May. The Preakness Stakes runs two weeks after the Kentucky Derby and Belmont Stakes runs three weeks after the Preakness Stakes. The distances? Kentucky Derby: a mile and a quarter. The Preakness Stakes: a mile and three-sixteenths (a sixteenth of a mile shorter than the Kentucky Derby). The Belmont Stakes: a mile and a half.

This is a grueling campaign which is why they call the final leg of the Triple Crown the Test of the Champion. Back up to the Kentucky Derby, and a mile and a quarter is the farthest any of these 3 year olds has ever run. They are then asked to come back in two weeks, a very quick turnaround, and shorten up to a mile and three-sixteenths, still racing against the very best of their generation. Then if they are to complete the Triple Crown they need to come back in three weeks, another relatively short turnaround, especially considering what they've endured thus far, and stretch out to a mile and a half. It's easy to see why the field size diminishes as this campaign goes on. While the Derby will generally have a capacity field of 20 horses, the Belmont Stakes is more likely to have six to eight.

Of course, not every horse that runs in the Derby is automatically assumed to come back in two weeks in the Preakness Stakes. The Preakness field will generally consist of the Derby winner and three to six horses from the Derby whose connections believe, for whatever reason, their chances of winning were compromised and they expect a better outcome in the Preakness. There will also be some "new shooters" in the Preakness Stakes, meaning horses that did not compete in the Derby generally because they did not have enough graded stakes earnings to get into that race or because they suffered a minor setback. Or sometimes a horse that is not ideally suited to the mile and a quarter distance of the Derby will take a shot at the slightly shorter distance of a mile and three-sixteenths. And, almost inevitably, there will be a local horse in the Preakness that has competed successfully over the Pimlico Race Course and is shooting for the stars in the Preakness. This race is generally not oversubscribed.

The Belmont Stakes suffers even more attrition because most American horses are not bred to relish the mile and a half distance and the horse with the most to gain from winning the Belmont Stakes is a horse that has won both the Kentucky Derby and the Preakness Stakes and is looking to add the third leg of the Triple Crown to his Crown of Jewels. Only 11 horses have ever won the Triple Crown. Many others have tried. And failed.

Beyond the Triple Crown, there are literally hundreds of other races for a 3 year old to compete in. Oftentimes the Kentucky Derby separates the pretenders from the contenders, and the connections of the "pretenders" get much more realistic with their goals for

KENTUCKY DERBY PARTIES

If you can't make it to the track then go to a Kentucky Derby party or have one. It's a great excuse to get the gang together while knowing you only need to really pay attention to the TV for two minutes. The first stop to make on your way to planning a Kentucky Derby party is www.KentuckyDerby.info. This is Churchill Downs' official Kentucky Derby website. Once there, click on "Kentucky Derby recipes" and "mint julep recipes." Your Derby party will not be complete without a mint julep station, roses, and some sort of wagering pool. If you're going to someone else's Derby party be sure to bring them roses and fresh mint for the juleps.

To be honest, I've never thrown a Kentucky Derby party or even been to one as I've either been at Churchill Downs or preferred to watch the race and the pre-race features without interruption or distraction. But it's very easy to find Derby party ideas on the Internet and on Churchill Downs' official Kentucky Derby website. I'll let you take it from here.

their horse after getting trounced in the Derby. As I said before, you have to be pretty good even to run in the Derby. But there is a cavernous amount of ground between "good" and "great."

The best 3 year olds will rest after the Triple Crown—briefly—then point for a late summer/fall campaign which will likely include a race or two at either Saratoga Race Course in Saratoga Springs, New York, or Del Mar Race Course in Del Mar, California. They will then point for a Breeders' Cup race in the fall and the very best will point for the Breeders' Cup Classic, which, at the time of this writing, carries with it a $5 million pot.

Many race beyond their 3-year-old year but the really good ones will retire to stallion duty.

At the end of the day, while very few horses actually make it as top stallions, it is the highest achievement of them all. A horse that wins the Derby and Breeders' Cup Classic, even if a victory in the latter comes the next season, that horse's stallion value increases exponentially.

Do fillies run in the Kentucky Derby?

Yes. But rarely. The Kentucky Oaks, run on the day before the Kentucky Derby, is the most prestigious horse race for 3-year-old fillies in North America. This race comes together much like the

Derby with prep races scattered throughout the United States, regional stars emerging, and then fillies meeting to compete on the Friday before the Kentucky Derby at Churchill Downs. If a filly is exceedingly precocious and has a sufficient amount of graded stakes earnings she is welcome to take on the boys, but it's a very tough task and one that only 40 fillies have ever tried in the entire history of the Kentucky Derby. Six of the 40 fillies to compete in the Kentucky Derby were post-time favorites, meaning more money was wagered on them than any of their competitors.

Three fillies have won the Kentucky Derby. Regret was the first to accomplish this feat back in 1915. It would be 65 years before this effort was duplicated when Genuine Risk won the Derby in 1980, and then just eight years later Winning Colors won the Derby in wire-to-wire fashion, meaning she led the field from start to finish. Winning Colors' Derby was the first Kentucky Derby that I witnessed live and to this day I cannot tell the story of her win and my experience of it without getting choked up. Suffice to say, she had every woman in attendance cheering her all the way to the wire and beyond. There were very few dry eyes in the house. Only three fillies have attempted the Run for the Roses since then and the best finish was second place.

Anyone who cares enough about racing to read this book and then read this far into this chapter has most likely heard of Rachel Alexandra and I'd be remiss not to mention her here. She's a filly who won the Kentucky Oaks by 20¼ lengths in a record-setting performance that left all in attendance in awe of how easily she demolished a very good field of contemporaries. After her romp in the Kentucky Oaks most racing enthusiasts believed her owners had chosen the wrong race for her and that she should have, instead, had a shot at the boys in the Kentucky Derby. Her owners felt otherwise and believed the Derby, Preakness, and Belmont Stakes races are races used to develop stallions and not suited for fillies.

A few days after her stunning performance in the Oaks Rachel Alexandra was privately purchased for an undisclosed amount of money (rumor has it at between $5 and $10 million) by business partners Jess Jackson and Harold McCormick who believed she indeed deserved a chance to run with the boys. Rachel Alexandra ran in the Preakness the following week and, true to her form, she ran like a girl. A fast one. The public made her the betting favorite and she rewarded her backers with a solid win over 12 of the best boys of her generation. Her connections declined to run her in the Belmont Stakes but her greatness had already been declared.

My first Kentucky Derby

Fittingly, the first Kentucky Derby I saw live was won by a filly: Winning Colors in 1988. She had won the Santa Anita Derby in the start prior to the Kentucky Derby so had already proven that she would be a formidable opponent for the boys. She was trained by D. Wayne Lukas and ridden by Gary Stevens and went to post as the co-betting favorite with a horse named Private Terms. Sixteen horses were entered against her.

Winning Colors' victory made an indelible impression.

At that time I was an apprentice jockey riding at Rockingham Park in New Hampshire but had been set down with a suspension for three days. My sister, Leah, who lives in Kentucky, was already planning to attend the Derby with friends and she encouraged me to fly into town and join them. It did not take much persuasion on her part.

We watched the Derby from the backside—the barn area— and I remember watching the horses leave from there as they made their way on to the track and then to the paddock and can recall thinking how amazing it was that I was seeing these grand animals up close and in person. Winning Colors was as big as any of the boys and bigger than most of them. She was a steel-gray filly who looked like a colt with the athletic frame and presence of a great horse. But many of her rivals were equally impressive. Forty Niner, Risen Star, Proper Reality, Seeking the Gold, Private Terms...16 boys. One girl.

I watched the race from atop one of the barns (which you could do at that time—this is no longer allowed) along the backstretch toward the second turn so I had a good view of the field racing toward me and a great view as they raced past me. Winning Colors took the lead from the start and as she led the field past me you could see she was still racing within herself (meaning she had plenty of energy left) and was alone on the lead by four lengths. That noted, I could also see that some of the boys had something left too, and Seeking the Gold, lying in second, was in dogged pursuit. As the field raced into the second turn my great view became not so good and I realized I would not be able to see the finish from my perch. As soon as the field raced past me I rushed to the TV set up just outside the barn to watch the finish.

By they time I got to the TV Seeking the Gold was beginning to tire and Winning Colors was still alone on the lead. Briefly. Forty Niner was now launching a massive rally and Risen Star was awakening from the back of the pack and making an equally impressive bid for the lead. At the top of the stretch (with a quarter mile left in the race) Winning colors was in front by three lengths. As the horses approached the eighth pole her lead rapidly diminished. I was watching this stretch run from a small TV surrounded by at least 20 people. There were 137,694 people at the track that day. And there was no one who was not screaming for Winning Colors to hold on to her lead. When the horses hit the wire she had held on by a neck and had carried the weight of every woman at the track that day. Emotions ran high. Forty Niner finished second. Risen Star finished two lengths back in third.

I'm happy to tell this story in this format because I've never been able to tell it in person without getting a lump in my throat and a tear in my eye and pausing to harness my emotions. I did no better writing about it. Winning Colors didn't just win the Kentucky Derby that day. She made every woman in attendance feel like a winner too. I will never forget that Derby. But, of course, if you ask around, everyone remembers his or her first Derby. Again, you just have to be there. You'll see what I mean.

BEYOND THE DERBY: OTHER GREAT RACES AND RACE DAYS

I think we've already established the Kentucky Derby as the clear-cut favorite in this category but, believe it or not, it's not the only great race and it's not the only great day to go to the races. Let's begin by backing up one day to the Kentucky Oaks.

In Louisville, Kentucky the Kentucky Oaks at Churchill Downs has become the locals' favorite day to go to the races. Yes, even preferable to going to the Kentucky Derby. First of all, it's very difficult to get a good ticket to the Derby, even if you live in Louisville. The race has become such a "must see" event that it's hard to see the race. It's just so crowded. And the tickets, if you can get one, are expensive. So many of the locals have resolved this problem by attending the races at Churchill Downs on Oaks Day,

The Kentucky Oaks always draws a large hometown crowd.

the day before the Derby, and then either having a Derby party the next day or going to one.

The Preakness Stakes, held just two weeks after the Kentucky Derby, is great because there is almost always a Triple Crown on the line. Barring injury or illness, the winner of the Kentucky Derby will run in the Preakness Stakes, the second leg of the Triple Crown. The Preakness is held at Pimlico Race Course in Baltimore, Maryland, and is a much more laid back affair than the Derby. Yes, people still dress up and yes, lots of the ladies still wear hats, but you'll see many, many people who come in jeans and a T-shirt, and the infield crowd is notoriously more rowdy than the infield crowd at the Derby. If you've ever been to the infield during the Kentucky Derby, you're probably asking, "You can get rowdier than that?" Yes. Yes, you can. Just go to the Preakness Stakes and you'll see what I'm talking about.

The Belmont Stakes is held three weeks after the Preakness Stakes and is run at Belmont Park in Elmont, New York, one of the many suburbs outside of the city. To be honest, the Belmont Stakes is only a great party if there's a Triple Crown on the line. If not, it's still a fun party but will pale in comparison to the first two legs. That said, it's still New York and if you love New York like I do, any excuse to go will work.

The Breeders' Cup has taken place every fall since its inception in 1984 but does not have a permanent date or a permanent host

The Preakness is the second leg of the Triple Crown.

track. It typically takes place on the last weekend of October or the first weekend of November. It's been contested at Arlington Park, Aqueduct, Belmont Park, Churchill Downs, Gulfstream Park, Hollywood Park, Lone Star Park, Monmouth Park, Santa Anita Park and Woodbine Racetrack and in 2007 went from being a one-day event to a two-day event.

Winning a Breeders' Cup race is a tremendous accomplishment.

The Breeders' Cup is different than any other big race day event in that it does not belong to a specific track and it does not center around one marquee race. The Breeders' Cup is the brainchild of the late John R. Gaines, a prominent Thoroughbred horse owner and breeder. His idea was to have an international event in the fall of the year with big races for all types of horses: fillies and colts, young horses and veteran campaigners, turf and dirt, sprinters and routers.

At the time he conceived it the biggest races ran in the spring and mid-summer and there was not much to look forward to in the racing world come fall. The Breeders' Cup would give owners and trainers a place to showcase talents in the fall and also give the racing world a much-needed boost at that time of year. As no one track owns the event and with the aim of making it fair to all who compete, it is moved annually to a different racetrack but one that is equipped to handle a big crowd and a big event.

As of this writing the Breeders' Cup now awards more than $25 million in purse money over the course of the two days. The biggest race is the Breeders' Cup Classic for 3 year olds and upward and contested at a mile and a quarter. In 2010, the Classic was worth $5 million. Winning this race is now almost as coveted as winning the Kentucky Derby, but the pinnacle is winning the Kentucky Derby in the spring and then the Breeders' Cup Classic in the fall.

The Breeders' Cup culminates the racing season, and many, many races take place in advance of this showcase of talent that decide who will be the favorites for the Breeders' Cup races. These lead-up races, if you will, are great races and race-day events too and, really, that's the point to this chapter. There are many fun days to attend the races and they generally center around a marquee race or racehorse.

Other big races

The Santa Anita Derby is a big deal at Santa Anita and in Southern California and it's a great day to attend the races. Same with the Florida Derby at Gulfstream Park, the Arkansas Derby at Oaklawn Park, the Louisiana Derby at the Fair Grounds, etc. The list goes on and on. Any of the Derby preps are going to be a good day of racing all around, but, generally speaking, the bigger the purse and more prestigious the grade, the bigger the day. Racetracks are very clever about throwing parties, though, so never underestimate the amount of fun you'll have based on the size of the purse.

The main tracks you need to visit in the United States are, in alphabetical order: Arlington, Belmont, Churchill Downs, Del Mar, Gulfstream, Keeneland, Santa Anita, and Saratoga. There are many, many more tracks and if they're having a big day of racing, go! You'll enjoy it. One of the biggest little parties I ever saw was in Tulsa, Oklahoma, at Fair Meadows when I flew in for the day to ride a stakes race (yes, a long time ago). And when I was a teenager the event we all looked forward to was the Cradle Stakes at River Downs racetrack near Cincinnati, Ohio. It was a fun day. Don't be a snob and start thinking you can only have fun at the really big events. A day at the races can be fun anytime.

When and where to go

Gulfstream Park in Hallandale Beach, Florida (between Ft. Lauderdale and South Beach, on the coast) opens toward the end of December or the first week of January and you can generally count on the track to throw a party for opening day or opening weekend.

In February the Derby preps begin so attending one of these prep races at Santa Anita, Gulfstream Park, Oaklawn Park, Turf Paradise (in Phoenix, Arizona), Tampa Bay Downs, Golden Gate, Turfway Park, or Sunland Park will likely be a good time.

In March the focus is still on Derby preps so stick with the tracks mentioned from February. If you have the means, Meydan Race Course in Dubai is amazing. It has its International Racing Carnival in February and March, culminating with Dubai World Cup Day in late March. Great horses from around the world. Men in top hats and coat tails with beautiful women in top European fashions and fabulous hats and Muslim men in their robes and ghutra head dressings. Here you'll find pomp and pageantry, spectacle and splendor, mixed with culture and competition. No wagering. It is all about the reverence of the horse. And the show.

In April you have to go to Keeneland Race Course on any day the Lexington track is racing and the sun is shining. Of course, their big racing days will be the busiest, and they can be so busy it's hard to move. Keeneland has two short meets a year: one in the spring and one in the fall.

In May it's all about the Derby and 3 year olds so Churchill Downs is the place to be on the first weekend in May. Pimlico Race Course in Baltimore, Maryland is where you'll want to be third weekend of May.

June brings us the Belmont Stakes from Belmont Park. This is three weeks after the Preakness Stakes so it falls on the first or second weekend of June. Even if there is not a Triple Crown on the line there will be other great races on the card to watch.

July, August, and early September we have summer racing at Del Mar, Saratoga Race Course, and Arlington Park. A day at the races at any of these three tracks on any day will be a lovely way to spend time with friends and family, and it's fun. Below is a short list of the best days to attend any of these three tracks. Like Derby Day and Breeders' Cup, there's much more to do than watch a horse race.

Saratoga's biggest day is Travers Stakes day in late August. The oldest major Thoroughbred race in the United States, the Travers, also known as the mid-summer Derby, is for 3 year olds and you'll generally find two or three of the favorites from that year's Kentucky Derby. This is one of three grade I races on the Travers Day card.

The Arlington Million contested at Arlington Park is a great event and takes place in August. Three grade I turf races, all on the same day, with the Arlington Million for 3 year olds and up worth... yes, you guessed it $1 million; the Beverly D for fillies and mares, also a grade I; and then the Secretariat Stakes for 3 year olds, all competed on the turf course.

Del Mar's biggest day takes place in early September and, while there are a few stakes races on the card, the day is highlighted by the $1 million Pacific Classic, a race for 3 year olds and up going a mile and a quarter.

September is bit of a slow month in racing as most of the good horses are now taking a break between their summer campaign and the Breeders' Cup.

In October Keeneland runs its fall meet. If you didn't get there in the spring, there's no bad day to go in the fall. Additionally, the Breeders' Cup will either be at the end of this month or the beginning of next month. Go to www.breederscup.com to find out when and where it will be.

November: If the Breeders' Cup didn't take place in October it will take place in November. Find it. Watch it or go. You'll be glad you did.

12

NAMES TO KNOW

I n the interest of keeping this book timely, the names of horses and people I mention are legends. Some are still active in the sport; many are long retired. I'll start with horses then move to trainers and jockeys. They are listed in alphabetical order so as not to infer partiality...with the lone exception of the first horse. Really, the only horse you just need to know.

Horses

Secretariat—One of only 11 horses to have won the Triple Crown. (You'll recall the Triple Crown is a sweep of the Kentucky Derby, Preakness Stakes, and Belmont Stakes.) Secretariat is the most often mentioned though and for two reasons: One, he was just so impressive in his annihilation of the competition and two, his Triple Crown sweep took place recently enough (1973) that many people remember seeing it. So, while in the history of horse racing there may have been a horse as impressive as Secretariat, seeing is always more impressive than hearing about it—or reading about it—and there has not been a horse as impressive as Secretariat since his racing career ended. Those who saw Secretariat remember him as a big, beautiful, strong, perfect physical specimen of an athlete who earned the nickname "Big Red." Secretariat won on any type of surface: fast track, sloppy track, and on the turf. After a successful racing career, Secretariat stood as a stallion at Claiborne Farm for many years. He died in 1989 at 19 years of age. In an ensuing autopsy Dr. Thomas Swerczek from the University of Kentucky estimated his heart weighed in at 22 pounds—nearly three times the size of the average Thoroughbred's heart!

In 2010 Disney released the movie *Secretariat*. As Hollywood and Disney are prone to do, they did take some creative liberties with this story. However, all of the significant and pertinent facts are depicted correctly and all of his human connections are very pleased with the movie, as was I. If you haven't seen it, you need to.

Affirmed—Affirmed is the most recent Triple Crown winner. He won in 1978 and was the third Triple Crown winner to come in the decade of the 1970s. He was ridden by a young, precocious jockey named Steve Cauthen who you'll read more about in the section on human legends.

Aristides—The first Kentucky Derby winner (1875).

Citation—One of only three horses you'll hear compared to Secretariat. He won the Triple Crown in 1948.

Rachel Alexandra—Earned the attention of everyone in the horse racing world when she won the Kentucky Oaks by 20¼ lengths in 2009. She earned the attention of nearly everyone in the world when she came back two weeks later to win the Preakness

Rachel Alexandra

Stakes, beating the best boys of her generation. Three months later she went on to beat older males in the Woodward Stakes at Saratoga Race Course, a feat no filly had ever achieved in the 56 runnings of that venerable race. It was a hard-fought victory for her, however, as she never really returned to top form after that race. She raced five more times, earning two more wins and three second-place finishes but her best races were long behind her. She retired healthy and sound in 2010 to live out the rest of her days as a broodmare. She'll be forever remembered as one of the best fillies of all time.

Man o' War—Considered the original "Big Red." Man o' War competed in 1919 and 1920 and won 20 of 21 races, including the Preakness Stakes, Belmont Stakes, and Travers Stakes among many others. He is ranked No. 1 on the Horses of the 20th

Century list and he's one of the three horses to which Secretariat is compared.

Seattle Slew—He won the Triple Crown in 1977.

Sir Barton—The first Triple Crown winner (1919).

War Admiral—Won the Triple Crown in 1937 and is one of only three horses that you'll hear compared to Secretariat.

Zenyatta—Will be remembered as one of the best horses of all time. She won her debut in November 2007 at age 3 and then went on to capture 18 consecutive wins. Those wins included victories in the 2008 Ladies Breeders' Cup Classic and the 2009 Breeders' Cup Classic (beating the boys). The latter race will forever be remembered by all who witnessed it.

She always dropped far back in the early stages of a race and then made a late charge, passing all of her rivals through the stretch. In the 2009 Classic she was simply too far back and appeared to be hopelessly beaten with an eighth of a mile left to go. Then she turned on the turbo. With enormous strides and the powerful surging body of a great athlete she turned the impossible into reality. She won the Classic—just barely—and filled the crowd with awe and reverence for the tremendous feat they had just witnessed.

She entered the 2010 Breeders' Cup Classic having gone 19 for 19. Perfect. She was just perfect. That year's Classic, however, handed her the only defeat of her admirable and peerless career.

Zenyatta poses in the winner's circle after the 2009 BC Classic.

She dropped back farther than ever in the early stages of the race and simply gave herself too much to do against a very talented horse named Blame. She made her patented late charge and she gave all she had. It just wasn't enough to win. For all who watched her race though, it was enough for her to remain perfect. OK, she was not 20 for 20. But she was still perfect. She retired healthy and sound after the 2010 Breeders' Cup classic and was expected to become a mom.

People—Trainers

Steve Asmussen—While Asmussen's accomplishments are surely notable, they may be more so because of his relatively young age. He started training horses in 1986 at age 20 (after a

brief career as a jockey—an occupation he soon outgrew) and in 2008, when he was just 43, he won 622 thoroughbred races, setting the single-season record by all horse trainers, past or present. In 2009 he broke his own record by winning 650 races on the year. He has won two Preakness Stakes and was the trainer of Rachel Alexandra. He has a very large stable of horses with divisions in the major racing states. It shouldn't be long before Asmussen is inducted into the National Museum of Racing and Hall of Fame.

Steve Asmussen

Bob Baffert—Baffert is a Southern California trainer who won his first Kentucky Derby in 1997 and by 2002 had won three Kentucky Derbies. He's also won five Preakness Stakes races and a Belmont Stakes. Baffert-trained horses have won two legs of the Triple Crown three different times (Real Quiet, 1998; Point Given, 2001; and War Emblem, 2002) but he has not managed to win the elusive Triple Crown. If you go to the races in Southern California, you need to know who Bob Baffert is. If you go to any of the Triple Crown races, you need to know who he is as well. In 2009 he was inducted into the National Museum of Racing and Hall of Fame.

Robert Frankel—Before the late Bobby Frankel became legendary in Southern California racing, he gained the attention

Friendly rivals: D. Wayne Lukas, left, and Bob Baffert

of the racing world with his dominance of New York racing. He began training in the mid 1960s and in the early '70s shifted the bulk of his racing stable to Southern California where he won as he pleased throughout the rest of his career. In 1995 he was inducted into the National Museum of Racing and Hall of Fame. He won only a single Triple Crown race—the Belmont Stakes in 2003 with Empire Maker—but he started relatively few horses in these classic races. His specialty was older horses, particularly older horses on the turf. Between 2001 and 2007 he won five Breeders' Cup races. He passed away in November 2009.

D. Wayne Lukas—More commonly known as Wayne Lukas. The "D" stands for Darrell but is never used. People refer to him as "Wayne" or "D. Wayne" but he introduces himself simply as "Wayne Lukas," and while he is clearly a legend he is also still actively training. He started out training Quarter Horses and switched to Thoroughbreds full time in 1978. He has won four Kentucky Derbies, five Preakness Stakes, and four Belmont Stakes, but has never won the Triple Crown. Incidentally, his first Derby win came in 1988 with the aforementioned Winning Colors. (His mark of 18 Breeder's Cup wins is a record for any trainer, jockey, or owner, and over the course of his career he has set many other money-earned and races-won records that will very likely never be broken. He has started a record 44 horses in the Kentucky Derby, 16 more than his nearest rival as such.

In 1999 he was inducted into the National Museum of Racing and Hall of Fame, and many of his top assistant trainers from over the years have gone on to train successfully on their own. They include Todd Pletcher, Dallas Stewart, Kiaran McLaughlin, Mark Henning, Mike Maker, Jerry Barton, and Randy Bradshaw.

Richard Mandella—Dick Mandella is a perennial top trainer on the Southern California circuit, and although he's never won a Triple Crown race he's had very few starters in the series. He has won every major stakes race worth winning in Southern California. In 2003 he set a Breeders' Cup record when he became the first trainer to win four Breeders' Cup races on one card. Two years prior to that Mandella was inducted into the National Museum of Racing and Hall of Fame.

Claude R. McGaughey III—Better known as Shug McGaughey (pronounced shoog mick-gay-he), this is a name you need to be familiar with if you're attending the races in New York or Gulfstream Park. McGaughey has been the private trainer for the powerful Phipps family since 1986. He won the Belmont Stakes in 1989 with the Phipps family-owned Easy Goer, and between 1988 and 2005 won nine Breeders' Cup races. In 2004 he was inducted into the National Museum of Racing and Hall of Fame. A native of Lexington, Kentucky, McGaughey has been racing in New York and South Florida since the early 1980s. He generally brings a small stable of horses to the Keeneland spring and fall meets and has earned six leading trainer titles at the Lexington track.

Bill Mott—Billy Mott is a name you need to be familiar with if you're going to the races in New York, Kentucky, or Florida. Like many top trainers today, he has a far-reaching stable of horses and is particularly known for his prowess with older horses, particularly older horses on the turf. He has won the Belmont Stakes once though has had relatively few starters in Triple Crown races. He has won six Breeders' Cup races and was inducted into the National Museum of Racing and Hall of Fame in 1998.

Todd Pletcher—Like Asmussen, Todd Pletcher is relatively young compared to his peers, especially when considering his accomplishments. He was a top assistant trainer for D. Wayne Lukas before going out on his own in 1995. By the spring of 2011 he was just 43 years old and had won 27 leading trainer titles at New York racetracks. Pletcher follows only his mentor, Lukas, in number of Kentucky Derby starters with a total of 29. In 2010 he won the Derby with Super Saver, a horse ridden by Calvin Borel and owned by WinStar Farm. He has won six Breeders' Cup races.

Nick Zito—Also referred to as "Derby Nick," Zito won his first Kentucky Derby in 1991 with Strike the Gold and then came back three years later to win again with Go For Gin. He has missed very few Kentucky Derbies since then, having started 24 horses in the Derby between

Todd Pletcher

1990 and 2010. He also owns a win in the Preakness Stakes and two in the Belmont Stakes. You need to know his name if you go to a Triple Crown race or to a track in New York. In 2005 he was inducted into the National Museum of Racing and Hall of Fame.

People—Jockeys

Patricia Barton—Retired. Patti Barton was one of the first half-dozen women to be licensed as a jockey in the United States. She began her career in 1969, and that year she won more races than any of her female competitors, making her the country's winningest female jockey. She had such a large lead in races won that she held that distinction until four years after her retirement

From left, Leah, Jerry, and Donna in the winner's circle with mother Patti

in 1984. She never won a Triple Crown race and, although she won many leading rider titles she never won one at any of the major tracks. She plied her trade at smaller tracks in and around the Midwest and the East Coast and was a big fish in a small pond, all the while paving the way for the female riders who would attempt to follow in her footsteps. She never tried moving to any of the major tracks because, as she says, she had a job to do that was even more important than riding: raising three kids. She was never inducted into the National Museum of Racing and Hall of Fame. So why is she here? Because she's my mother and I'm proud of her. And this is my book.

Jerry Bailey—Retired. Jerry was a dominant force in New York's horse racing game from the early 1990s through his retirement in 2006. Between 1991 and 2005 he won the Kentucky Derby three times, the Preakness Stakes twice, the Belmont Stakes twice, and still holds the record for the most Breeders' Cup wins with 15, five of which came in the Breeders' Cup Classic. He also won the world's richest race, the Dubai World Cup, four times. He was inducted into the National Museum of Racing Hall of Fame in 1995. As of this writing he is an on-air horse racing analyst for ABC Sports and ESPN.

Steve Cauthen—Retired. Also known as Stevie. He started his career in 1976 at River Downs, a small racetrack along the river near Cincinnati, Ohio, and quickly moved on to national prominence. In 1977 he set a single-season earnings record for a jockey when horses he rode earned $6 million in purse money and the following year, at just 18 years of age, he became the youngest jockey ever to win the Triple Crown when he accomplished the feat aboard Affirmed.

He was known as much for his soft demeanor and good manners as he was for his skill with a horse. Horses just ran for him. In 1979 he moved his tack to England where the scale of riding weights is higher than in the United States. After all, he was still a growing boy when his career began—and he was still growing. He retired from riding in 1993 after years of battling to keep his weight below the ideal for his physique. He will forever be revered by the racing public and always remembered as the boy with ice water in his veins for his tactical rides aboard Affirmed in the Triple Crown series. In 1994 he was inducted into the National

Museum of Racing and Hall of Fame.

Angel Cordero, Jr.—Retired. Between 1974 and 1985 Angel won three Kentucky Derbies, two Preakness Stakes, and two Belmont Stakes. Cordero also won four Breeder's Cup races. Cordero will always be remembered as one of the best jockeys ever to ride in New York, one of the toughest racing circuits in the United States. He was a risk taker with a big personality who was outgoing and friendly but never afraid to fight for what he believed in. He was inducted into the National Museum of Racing and Hall of Fame in 1988.

Pat Day

Pat Day—Retired. Between 1984 and 2001 Pat Day won the Kentucky Derby, five Preakness Stakes races, three Belmont Stakes races, and 12 Breeders' Cup races including four Breeders' Cup Classics (the biggest purse in North America). In 1991 he was inducted into the National Museum of Racing and Hall of Fame. From the 1980s until his retirement in 2005 Day dominated horse racing in the Midwest, particularly at Churchill Downs, Keeneland, and Arlington Park.

Julie Krone—Retired. She first retired in 1999 as the leading female jockey in the United States by both races won and money earned. By that time she had distinguished herself as the only female jockey to have won a Triple Crown race, winning the Belmont Stakes on Colonial Affair in 1993. Beyond that, she had stamped herself as one of the most talented and formidable riders

Julie Krone

on the East Coast and before retiring won leading rider titles at Belmont Park, Gulfstream Park, Monmouth Park, Meadowlands, and Atlantic City Race Course. In 2000 she was inducted into the National Museum of Racing and Hall of Fame, the first woman ever honored with such distinguished recognition.

Krone then came out of retirement in 2002 and dominated horse racing in Southern California much as she had in

New York. In 2003 she became the first female jockey to win a Breeders' Cup race, winning the Juvenile Fillies on Halfbridled. In December 2003 she was badly injured in a racing accident. She returned to riding in February 2004 but only for a day, after which she made a statement that did not include an official proclamation of retirement but suggested she may never ride competitively again.

In 2008 she was asked to participate in a "Legends" race consisting solely of retired Hall of Fame jockeys. She accepted the invitation to ride with Jerry Bailey, Angel Cordero, Jr., Pat Day, Sandy Hawley, Chris McCarron, Gary Stevens, and Jacinto Vasquez. Sandy Hawley won the race easily. As of this writing Krone has not participated in another Thoroughbred race.

Chris McCarron—Retired. Chris McCarron started riding in Maryland in 1974 and immediately took the racing world by storm. He shifted his tack to the more prestigious Southern California racetracks in 1977, the same year he won his first of three Kentucky Oaks races. He went on to win two Kentucky Derbies, two Preakness Stakes, two Belmont Stakes, and nine Breeders' Cup races including five Breeders' Cup Classic races. In 1989 he was inducted into the National Museum of Racing and Hall of Fame.

Chris McCarron

He retired from riding professionally in 2002, then in 2003 served as a technical advisor, racing designer, and actor in the popular film *Seabiscuit*. In 2006 he opened the very first school for future jockeys in North America at the Kentucky Horse Park in Lexington, Kentucky.

William Shoemaker—Retired and deceased. One of the greatest jockeys of all time. Referred to as Bill, Willie, or "The Shoe," he was a very small man (yes, even by jockey standards) with an enormous gift. Horses just ran for him. He was a diminutive 4'11" and weighed just 95 pounds but those who knew him figured at least 10 percent of his body weight consisted of his enormous heart. He rode from 1949 until 1990 and won four Kentucky Derbies, two Preakness Stakes, and five Belmont Stakes.

As jockeys go, he suffered very few injuries so it was particularly ironic that he was paralyzed in an automobile accident a year after he retired from riding. He went on to train horses until he retired from that too in 1997. He passed away in 2003 and will forever be revered by those who knew him.

Gary Stevens—Retired. Gary Stevens won his first Kentucky Derby in 1988 and then went on to win two more Kentucky Derby runnings, two Preakness Stakes, three Belmont Stakes, and eight Breeders' Cup races. For a 20-year span starting in the 1980s, Stevens could always be found at the top of the jockey's standings on the very tough Southern California. His domination in California was so strong that he won the Santa Anita Derby a record eight times. In 1997 he was inducted into the National Museum of Racing and Hall of Fame.

In 2003 he played the role of George Wolfe in the popular *Seabiscuit* movie. He retired from riding in 2005 and, as of this writing, works as an on-air horse racing analyst for NBC Sports and HRTV, a horse racing network.

Owners and breeders

Owners and breeders are so vital to horse racing that in order to list all of the important names I'd have to include nearly every person who has ever owned or currently owns a Thoroughbred. Owning racehorses is a risky proposition with many expenses, many heartbreaks, and only a few really meaningful awards and

The late Jess Jackson delighted in winning an Eclipse Award.

rewards. Luckily for all of us, the thrill of winning is enough to keep them in the game because, without them, the sport would cease to exist.

Awards

Induction into the National Museum of Racing and Hall of Fame is clearly the highest level of achievement and recognition in Thoroughbred racing but it is an honor, not an award. In Thoroughbred horse racing there is only one award that really matters: the Eclipse Award. Nearly every horse, trainer, and jockey listed above has received an Eclipse Award at some point in his or her career.

The Eclipse Award is racing's equivalent to the Academy Award (or Oscar) in the film industry or the Tony Award in American theater. As with these other prestigious awards, there are many categories for the Eclipse: owners, breeder, training, jockey, apprentice jockey, Horse of the Year, etc.

I mention this only so you know that if you see the Hall of Fame Eclipse Award designation before the name of a trainer or jockey, that's a pretty big deal, in our game, anyway.

My Favorite Tracks

I f you've read everything in this book by now it's not hard to tell which are my favorite tracks. So this chapter will be short, consisting of my top five favorite tracks and what I like about them.

No. 1 **Keeneland Race Course**: Why: Not only is Keeneland one of the top tracks in the United States, it has a long history of great horse racing and you can't help but feel the presence of champions past and present just by walking onto the haloed grounds. Keeneland has the biggest purses too, and big purses attract good horses and good horses attract big crowds. Plus,

Keeneland has history, good racing, and enthusiastic fans.

Keeneland is in Lexington, Kentucky, which is not only the home to some of the top Thoroughbred breeding farms in the world but also the home to the University of Kentucky as well as some of the wealthiest Kentuckians in the state. On any given day—even weekdays—Keeneland will be packed wall to wall with people of all ages and stages gathering to have fun with their friends, bet some races, and watch some of the best horses in the country compete in head-to-head battle.

Additionally, Keeneland only runs two short meets a year, one in the spring and one in the fall, so they never oversaturate their customers with too much of a good thing. In fact, people just can't get enough of Keeneland.

Keeneland is unique in that it generates most of its money from the Thoroughbred horse sales it conducts throughout the year. Auction proceeds go back into purses, the facility, and the community as Keeneland has a long tradition of supporting non-profit organizations and causes.

No. 2 **Saratoga Race Course**: Why: Like Keeneland, Saratoga has a long history of great horse racing, great horses, and exciting people attending the races. Saratoga is older than the Kentucky Derby. It first opened in 1863 and is the oldest organized sporting venue of any kind in the United States. Also called the Spa for the nearby mineral spas, Saratoga Race Course is in Saratoga Springs in upstate New York. In the late 1800s and early 1900s many of New York City's wealthiest residents built summer homes here. The Saratoga meet began as a four-day meet in 1863 and now runs for six weeks. Saratoga Springs is still the summer home to many wealthy people, especially those who own horses or appreciate great horse racing.

Saratoga Race Course is still very organic in nature. For the most part it is not air-conditioned and even the very wealthy sit outdoors in "boxes" that have been in their families for generations. But it is also very family friendly and on the big days you'll see people lined up outside of the admission gates waiting for the gates to open so that they can rush inside and lay claim to a picnic table or grassy knoll where they'll set up "camp" for the day's races.

It is also unique in that it is the only major racetrack in the United States where the jockeys have to walk right through the crowd after the race to get back to the jock's room (the slang term we use for the jockeys' quarters), making it a great place for children and/or racing fans to obtain autographs.

No. 3 **Arlington Park**: Why: Arlington Park is young compared to Saratoga and did not officially open until 1927 but at that time Chicago was a popular hub for great horse racing. The Arlington Park of today bears no resemblance to the first Arlington Park built as the original track burned to the ground in 1985. Fortunately the fire started in the very early morning and no lives were lost. In 1989 the "new and improved" Arlington Park re-opened, debuting one of the grandest and most beautiful racetracks ever built in the United States. Arlington Park's six-story grandstand and clubhouse are really sights to behold, though the picnic areas with open grass and open seating are just as beautiful and inviting. Aside from the splendor of the racetrack, Arlington Park is just outside of the fabulous city of Chicago, giving you *two* great excuses to visit the area.

No. 4 **Del Mar Racetrack**: Why: Had I spent more time on the West Coast this may have been my favorite track. Del Mar, where "the surf meets the turf," lies on the Pacific coast just north of San Diego so it is centered on prime real estate offering more than just great horse racing as a compelling reason to visit the track. But you will find great horse racing.

Del Mar first opened in 1937 with Bing Crosby at the entrance gate to meet and greet fans, and by 1940 it was the summer

Del Mar: "where the surf meets the turf"

Churchill Downs is special on big-event days.

stomping ground for many of Hollywood's biggest stars. Its star power has not diminished since. It runs for just 37 days, from mid-July to early September, but contests nearly 20 graded stakes races during that short span. At Del Mar you'll find North America's top jockeys and trainers mingling with some of Hollywood's biggest stars, all there to watch or participate in some of the best horse racing in the world. What's not to like? Oh, and the weather? Perfect.

No. 5 **Churchill Downs**: Why: With all my talk of the "must see" Kentucky Derby, I'm sure many of you would have thought this to be my No. 1 choice, and maybe it should have been. But day-in and day-out racing at Churchill Downs is not nearly as spectacular as racing on Kentucky Oaks and Kentucky Derby days, and the fact is, while the enormous facility is perfect for big events like the Derby and Breeders' Cup, it can seem a bit cavernous on a normal Wednesday.

That said, Churchill Downs is still a spectacular racetrack with a well of racing history and a top-notch group of jockeys and trainers racing there every day they run. Additionally, the Kentucky Derby Museum adjoins the track, so a visit to both is easily accomplished.

GLOSSARY OF RACING TERMS

Many of these terms are not used in this book but it's very likely that if you go to the track you'll hear these words and wonder what they mean.

Agent—Represents a jockey and handles his/her racing business. Jockey agents handle business for only one or two jockeys.

Allowance race—An event other than claiming for which the racing secretary drafts certain conditions.

Apprentice—A novice jockey, also called a bug rider. Apprentices get a 10-pound weight allowance over their fellow riders. The weight allowance decreases to five pounds as the number of wins increases. An apprenticeship ends a year from the date of the fifth winning ride.

Apprentice allowance—Weight concession to an apprentice rider. This varies among states from five to 10 pounds. Slang term is "bug." Indicated by an asterisk next to the jockey's name in the program.

Apron—The paved area in front of the grandstand and clubhouse and abutting to the track.

Backside—A racetrack's barn or stable area.

Backstretch—The straight part of the track on the far side between turns; slang term to describe the barn or stable area.

Back up—To walk or jog clockwise around the racetrack. Horses gallop, work, and race counter-clockwise.

Balk—To shy away or refuse to move forward.

Barrel—A horse's rib cage.

Bay—A horse's coat color ranging from tan to auburn. The mane and tail are always black as are the lower portion of the legs (black points), except for any white markings.

Bit—A metal or rubber device attached to the bridle and placed in the horse's mouth.

Blinkers—A cupped attachment to the bridle that prevents a horse from seeing to the side and rear.

Bolt—When a horse swerves sharply to the left or right.

Breeze—(See work.)

Bug boy—An apprentice jockey.

Bug—Another term for an apprentice jockey. (See Apprentice.) The term "bug" rider came about because of the bug-like appearance asterisk * that is used in the program placed next to the weight assignment of an apprentice jockey, i.e., 112*. The asterisk denotes that the horse is getting a weight allowance because an apprentice jockey will be riding. One asterisk denotes a five-pound weight allowance, two asterisks denote a seven-pound allowance, and three asterisks denote a 10-pound allowance. The more asterisks, the less experience the jockey has had.

Bridle—A head harness used for guiding horses. It consists of a headstall, bit, and reins.

Calls—An agreement between a jockey's agent and a trainer that promises the jockey will ride that trainer's horse and that the trainer will use that jockey. Calls are expected to be honored.

Card—The day's races.

Chestnut—A horse's coat color ranging from golden to red to chocolate (liver chestnut). Mane and tail are usually the same shade as the body; also, a small, horny growth on the inside of a horse's legs, just above the knee on the forelegs and below the hocks on the hind legs.

Claiming race—An event in which each horse entered can be purchased at a set price. Not just anyone can purchase these horses. You have to be a licensed owner and have run a horse at that meet.

Clerk of scales—A racing official whose job it is to weigh in the riders before and after each race to make sure the assigned weight is carried by the horse.

Colors—The racing silks worn by jockeys in races. The silks, or colors, belong to the owner of the horse and uniquely identify that stable.

Conformation—The shape and correctness of a horse's anatomy.

Cross—Changing the position of the reins so one rein will cross over another, allowing a rider either to tighten or loosen his hold by merely loosening the "cross" or by reeling in more rein. You'll hear people at the track say, "He didn't even hit his horse; he just kept throwing crosses."

Coupled—Two or more horses running as a single betting unit. Also known as an entry.

Cut—When a horse takes off at a dead run; also refers to a horse having been gelded or castrated.

Daily double—A type of wager calling for the selection of the winners of two consecutive races, usually the first and second on the race card.

Dark day—A day when the track does not race. It is like the weekend or a day off for those who work at the racetrack.

Derby—A stakes race for 3 year olds.

Double call—When a jockey has two calls from different trainers in one race.

Draw—Each horse entered into a race needs to have a post position, which is also the number on its saddle cloth. The names of each entered horse are placed in a file and pulled out along with a numbered plastic ball from a non-transparent bottle. The number on the ball decides from which position the horse will break and generally determines the horse's number except in the case of a dual entry. (See dual entry.)

Dual entry—Often referred to simply as an "entry." It is two horses entered into the same race that are owned by the same owner. These horses run as an "entry," such as 1 and 1A, 2 and 2B, etc. In this case, their number does not always accurately reflect their post-position.

Entries—Horses entered into a race.

Exacta—To win, a bettor must pick the horses that finish first and second in exact order.

Exercise rider—Riders who gallop, work, and ride racehorses during morning training.

Feature race—The best and richest race of the day, and usually run as the second to last race on the card.

Field—The entire group of horses competing in a race.

Filly—A female Thoroughbred that has not reached her fifth birth date or has not been bred.

Flak jacket—(See vest.)

Furlong—One-eighth of a mile, 220 yards, or 660 feet.

Futurity—A race specifically for 2 year olds.

Gate—A metal set of stalls into which the horses are loaded and confined until the front doors of every stall spring open simultaneously at the start of each race. A bell connected to the gate rings a fraction of a second after the stall doors open.

Gelding—Male horse that has been castrated.

Graded stakes—The highest caliber of stakes races. Grade I is the most prestigious, followed by grade II and grade III.

Groom—A person who cares for the horses in a stable.

Gray—A horse's coat color that is composed of a mixture of black and white hairs. Beginning with foals of 1993, The Jockey Club classifies a gray horse as "gray/roan."

Handicap—A race in which the racing secretary determines the weight each horse will carry according to his assessment of the horse's ability relative to the other horses in the field. The better the horse the more weight he would carry to give each horse a theoretically equal chance of winning.

Handicapper—One who handicaps races, officially or privately; expert who makes selections for publication. Also, name given to the racing secretary who assigns weights for handicaps at his track. Also, a horse that usually runs in handicap races.

Hands—A horse's height is measured in hands. One hand equals four inches. Thoroughbreds are typically 15 to 17 hands tall. Their height is measured from the ground to the withers.

High weight—Highest weight assigned or carried in a race.

Hot walker—A person who walks the horse after a workout or race until the horse's heart rate slows down and its body temperature cools.

In the money—When a horse finishes first, second, or third.

Journeyman—After completing an apprenticeship, a rider is considered a journeyman. Journeymen are experienced riders.

Knot—Bridles for Thoroughbred racehorses come with extra-long reins so they can fit any size horse. Jockeys and exercise riders can shorten them by tying a knot. Knots also prevent the reins, if they are ever dropped or the horse becomes loose, from becoming entangled in the horse's legs.

Length—A measurement approximating the length of a horse from nose to tail, about eight feet. Distance between horses in a race; calculated as one-fifth of a second in terms of time.

Live mount—A term to describe a jockey's mount if it has a very good chance to win.

Maiden—A horse that has never won a race.

Mare—A female Thoroughbred 5 years old or older, or younger if she has been bred.

Morning line—Odds quoted in the official program at the track and are the odds at which betting opens.

Mutuel pool—Pari-mutuel pool; sum of the wagers on a race or event, such as the win pool, exacta pool, etc.

Mutuel window—Place at a racetrack or other betting facility where a person goes to make a wager or to collect winnings.

Nominate—Declaring your intent to run in a stakes race. Sometimes a nomination fee must be paid by the owner.

Oaks—A stakes event for 3-year-old fillies.

Objection—Claim of foul lodged by one jockey against another.

Off the board—Describes a horse that finishes worse than third.

On the board—Describes a horse that finishes first, second, or third.

Out of the money—A horse that finishes worse than third.

Outrider—A person mounted on a pony whose job it is to watch out for any possible trouble on the racetrack and help the rider or loose horse as best they can.

Paddock—The area in which the horses are saddled and paraded around before post time.

Pari-mutuel—Form of wagering at all U.S. tracks today in which odds are determined by the amount of money bet on each horse. In essence, bettors are competing against each other and not against the track, which acts as an agent, taking a commission on each bet to cover purses, taxes, and operating expenses.

Past performances—A line-by-line listing of a horse's race record, plus earnings, connections, bloodlines, and other pertinent information.

Pedigree—A written record of a Thoroughbred's immediate ancestors.

Place—To finish second in a race. Placing a bet to "place" means that you are betting that the horse will run no worse than second. You win the bet if the horse runs first or second.

Pole—Markers placed at measured distances around the track and identified by distance from the finish line; i.e., the quarter pole is a quarter of a mile from the finish.

Pony—Pony refers to the horses that accompany Thoroughbreds to the starting gate. This term is a bit improper because a pony actually is a horse that stands no taller than 14.2 hands, such as a Shetland pony. The horses used as lead ponies during a post parade or for problematic or overly anxious racehorses during morning workouts are generally retired Thoroughbred racehorses, Quarter Horses, or other more docile breeds.

Pony person—A person on a pony that escorts the racehorse and jockey onto the track and through the post parade.

Post parade—Horses going from the paddock to the starting gate (post), parading past the stands.

PPs—(See past performances.)

Prep (or prep race)—Training; an event that precedes another, more important, engagement.

Program—A printed booklet of the scheduled races for a given day that lists each entered horse, the jockeys, trainers, owners, the assigned weights, and the time each race is to run.

Purse—The prize money for a race. It is divided up among the top five finishers, with the winning horse receiving the largest share, usually about 60 percent.

Quarter—One-quarter of a mile, 440 yards, or 1,320 feet.

Racing office—An office where the racing officials work, such as stewards, racing secretary, and entry clerks. This is also where entries are taken, the draw is conducted, and much of racing's business takes place.

Roan—A horse's coat color that is a mixture of red and white hairs or brown and white hairs. The Jockey Club classifies this coat color under the label "gray/roan."

Run-out bit—A bit made specifically to prevent a horse from either bearing out or in so that the horse will run straight.

Saddle cloth—Cloth under the saddle on which the number denoting the horse's post position is displayed for races.

Scale of weights—Fixed imposts to be carried by horses in a race, determined according to age, sex, season, and distance.

Shank—Rope or lead that is attached to the halter by which a horse is led.

Show—To finish third. Placing a bet to "show" means the horse you pick can run first, second, or third and you still win your bet.

Six furlongs—Three-quarters of a mile, 1,320 yards, or 3,960 feet.

Sixteenth—One-sixteenth of a mile, 110 yards, or 330 feet.

Sloppy (track)—Condition of track surface in which it is saturated with water and standing water is visible.

Slow (track)—Condition of track surface in which the surface and base are both wet.

Soft (track)—Condition of the turf course with a large amount of moisture.

Snaffle bit—Also referred to as a D-bit. It is the basic bit and most often used on young horses. It is a sufficient bit to start most young horses in and is used for horses that guide well.

Sprint—A race distance of less than one mile in Thoroughbred racing.

Stakes—The highest class of race. A race in which an entry fee is paid by

the owners of the horses starting and those entry fees are added to the purse; thus, a stakes is often referred to as an added-money race. Often all such entry fees go to the winner. Entry fees are not required for any other type of race including "overnight" stakes races which are non-graded and have a purse that is only slightly more than an allowance race. Also, invitational races (no entry fee required) with a large purse (usually $50,000 or more) are regarded as stakes races.

Stand out—The process of allowing a horse to stand next to the outside rail while facing the inside rail. They stand there and watch other horses train. It is a technique used to quiet a horse and let it get used to new surroundings. Also, a clear favorite in a race. Can also be referred to as a stick out.

Starter—The person responsible for pressing a button that opens all of the stall doors of the starting gate simultaneously at the start of each race. It is this person's job to make sure each horse gets a fair break.

Stewards—Racing officials who uphold the rules of racing at a racetrack. They answer to the state racing commission and their decisions can be appealed to that body.

Stretch—Homestretch; straightaway portion of a racetrack in front of the grandstand.

Switching leads—When a horse gallops or races, the horse leads with either its left or right foreleg. A racehorse should be on its right lead when running down a straight away and on its left lead going around a turn.

Tack—The equipment, such as a saddle, bridle, boots, helmet, vest, etc., that is used to ride a horse.

Tattoo—Letters and numbers imprinted on the inside of a racehorse's upper lip. These markings identify that horse exactly with his registered papers. A horse must be tattooed before it will be allowed to race.

Thoroughbred—Horses specifically bred for racing that can trace their lineage back to three original sires: Darley Arabian, Godolphin Arabian, and Byerley Turk.

Tongue tie—A piece of cloth or bandage used to tie down a horse's tongue to prevent the tongue from getting over the bit during a race or workout. If a horse gets its tongue over the bit that makes it very difficult to steer it effectively.

Totalizator—Machine that sells betting tickets; records total of win, place, and show pools; and keeps track of the amount bet on each horse in the three categories; shows odds to win on each horse in the field and

complete payoffs after the finish.

Tote board—The electronic totalizator display in the infield, which presents up-to-the-minute odds. It also may show the amounts wagered in each mutuel pool as well as information on jockey and equipment changes, etc.

Track bias—A racing surface that seems to favor a particular running style, such as front-running, or position, such as the rail.

Track record—Fastest time at various distances at a particular course.

Trainer—The person who conditions and prepares horses for racing.

Triple Crown—Three specific grade I races: the Kentucky Derby, Preakness Stakes, and Belmont Stakes. The Kentucky Derby is always run on the first Saturday in May. The Preakness runs two weeks later. The Belmont runs three weeks after the Preakness.

Turf course—A grass race course.

Undercard—Every race card has a feature race or feature races and an undercard. The feature race or races have the largest purses and the undercard consists of every other race on the card.

Under wraps—A horse being kept under strong restraint during a workout or while running in a race.

Valet—Person who attends to, cleans, and arranges the jockey's tack and wardrobe and helps trainers to saddle their horses in the paddock before races. At the racetrack valet is pronounced "val-let."

Vest—A vest made of dense, lightweight, padding that weighs less than two pounds but offers some protection if a rider is kicked, stepped on, or thrown from a horse. These vests are often referred to as flak jackets.

Withers—The place where the base of a horse's neck meets its back and where the spine begins. This is the horse's center of gravity and where it is best able to balance weight placed on its back. This is where the front of the saddle should be placed.

Work—Faster than a gallop but usually slower than race speed. Horses must work every few days to obtain and/or maintain their fitness level for racing. The trainer decides how far the horse will work. Often times a work is also referred to as a "breeze."

Win—To finish first. Placing a bet to "win" means your horse must win in order to win your bet.

Wire to wire—When a horse is in front from the gate to the finish line.

Yielding—Condition of the turf course with a lot of moisture in it causing horses to sink into it noticeably.

REFERENCES

Horse Racing Book, Periodical, DVD and Movie Guide

The sport of horse racing has so many subplots that it's impossible to cover the scope of this subject in any *one* book. This list of books written about horse racing, racehorses, jockeys, trainers, owners, and wagering is meant as a nice starting point if you wish to learn more about any of these elements. This is *by no means* a comprehensive list. If I tried to do that it would take up more space than all of the contents of this book.

As a former jockey there's no question I'm partial to other jockeys' stories. But one of the reasons why I'll start with them is because in reading about a particular jockey's story—or even a compilation of several jockeys' stories— you're less likely to be bombarded with esoteric terms. Let's get started.

Books about Jockeys

The Kid by Pete Axthelm. New York, NY: Bantam Books, 1978. A book I read growing up. It's about Steve Cauthen and how he went from an obscure racetrack in Ohio to the cover of *Sports Illustrated*.

The Shoe: Willie Shoemaker's Illustrated book of Racing by William Shoemaker and Dan Smith. Chicago, IL: Rand McNally and Company, 1976. The wonderful story of legend Bill Shoemaker. Born prematurely and kept in a shoebox in the oven to stay warm for the first few days of his life, he went on to become one of the greatest jockeys of all time.

Ride of Their Lives: The Triumphs and Turmoil of Today's Top Jockeys by Lenny Shulman. Lexington, KY: Eclipse Press, 2002. A bit dated now but still a good book about many of the top riders in the late 1990s and early 2000s.

Riding For My Life by Julie Krone and Nancy Ann Richardson. Boston, MA: Little, Brown and Company, 1995. I read this book without ever putting it down. Not because it's that short, but because it was that good. Julie was an amazing athlete with an almost psychic ability to get into a horse's head. Her interest in horses began as a very young child and has never waned. She is not officially retired but has not ridden since 2004. She lives in Southern California and is a very dear friend.

The Perfect Ride by Gary Stevens and Mervyn Kaufman. New York, NY: Kensington Publishing Corp., 2002. The story of Hall of Fame jockey Gary Stevens, who is now retired and covers horse racing for NBC Sports and HRTV.

Against The Odds: Riding For My Life by Jerry Bailey and Tom Pedulla. New York, NY: The Penguin Group, 2005. A seemingly candid look at the trials and tribulations that Bailey experienced on his way to becoming leading jockey in the United States.

The Lady is a Jock by Lynn Haney. Cornwall, NY: The Cornwall Press, Inc., 1973. A very old book that tells the stories of many of the female jockey pioneers. It was not written as a history on the first female jockeys but rather as a reference book for school libraries. My mother, Patti Barton, has a chapter in this book.

Sport of Kings: America's Top Women Jockeys Tell Their Stories Edited by Scooter Toby Davidson and Valerie Anthony. Syracuse, NY: Syracuse University Press, 1999. A book that's also a bit dated but contains the stories of many of the leading female jockeys at that time. There is a chapter on this author (under my maiden name, Donna Barton) and my photo is on the cover.

Books about Horse Trainers and Training a Race Horse

The Training Game by Karen M. Johnson. New York, NY: Daily Racing Form Press, 2008. This book is written by a woman whose father trained horses for a very long time in New York (P. G. Johnson) so she has an inside track to the people whose stories she so adeptly tells. In this book you'll read the stories of trainers Steve Asmussen, Rick Dutrow, Bobby Frankel, Neil Howard, Allen Jerkens, Carl Nafzger, Todd Pletcher, and Nick Zito.

Baffert: Dirt Road to the Derby by Bob Baffert and Steve Haskin. Lexington, KY: The Blood-Horse, Inc., 1999. Bob Baffert's sort of rags-to-riches story written by Baffert and one of my all-time favorite turf writers, Steve Haskin.

Traits of a Winner by Carl Nafzger. Neenah, WI: The Russell Meerdink Company, Ltd., 1994. Author, Carl Nafzger, has won the Kentucky Derby twice.

Books about Wagering

Blood-Horse Authoritative Guide to Betting Thoroughbreds. Lexington, KY.: Eclipse Press, A Division of Blood-Horse Publications, 2005.

Betting Thoroughbreds: For the 21st Century by Steve Davidowitz. New York, NY: Daily Racing Form Press, 2009.

Betting Synthetic Surfaces by Bill Finley. New York, NY: Daily Racing Form Press, 2008.

Expert Handicapping: Winning Insights into Betting Thoroughbreds by Dave Litfin. New York, NY: Daily Racing Form Press, 2007 (revised).

Beyer on Speed by Andrew Beyer. Boston, MA: Houghton Mifflin Co., 1993.

The Body Language of Horses by Tom Ainslie and Bonnie Ledbetter. Harper Collins, 1980. This book is also available on DVD—*The Body Language of the Racehorse*, with former jockey Chris McCarron.

Books about Great Thoroughbreds

Thoroughbred Champions: Top 100 Racehorses of the 20th Century by the staff and correspondents of *The Blood-Horse*. Lexington, KY: Eclipse Press, 1999.

Big Red of Meadow Stable: Secretariat, the Making of a Champion by William Nack. New York, NY: Arthur Fields Books, Inc. 1975. Author Bill Nack also played an advisory role in the making of the movie *Secretariat* produced by Walt Disney Productions.

Barbaro: The Horse Who Captured America's Heart by Sean Clancy. Lexington, KY: Eclipse Press, 2007. I haven't read this book as I was already well versed in the story of Barbaro. However, author Sean Clancy is one of my favorite writers and I'm certain his depiction of the Barbaro story is a fun and informative read.

Ruffian: Burning From the Start by Jane Schwartz. New York, NY: Ballantine Books, 1991. Ruffian is one of the best racing mares of all time and though it's been many years since I read this book, the subject matter makes this a thrilling story.

Eclipse: The Horse – The Race – The Awards by Michael Church. London: Thoroughbred Advertising, 2000. In theater they have the Tony Awards. In Hollywood they have the Emmys and the Oscars. In horse racing we have the Eclipse Awards named after the great racehorse, Eclipse. In this book you'll learn about the horse, his exploits, and the awards.

Seabiscuit: An American Legend by Laura Hillenbrand. New York, NY: Random House, 2001. A great book about a great horse and the inspiration for the movie *Seabiscuit*.

Other Books

Women in Racing: In Their Own Words by John and Julia McEvoy. Lexington, KY: Eclipse Press, 2001. A father and daughter writing duo teamed to tell some of the great stories of women in racing—and from all areas of racing, not just jockeys, trainers or owners.

The Great Black Jockeys: The Lives and Times of the Men Who Dominated America's First National Sport by Edward Hotaling. Rocklin, CA: Prima Publishing, 1999.

DVDs and Movies about Horse Racing

Thoroughbred, DVD. A documentary about the Thoroughbred and sport of horse racing produced and directed by Paul Wagner. The DVD can be ordered from Kentucky Educational Television (KET) by calling 1-800-945-9167 or visiting www.ket.org.

The Body Language of the Racehorse, DVD. Narrated by former jockey and Racing Hall of Fame member, Chris McCarron, and co-author of the book, *The Body Language of the Horse*, Bonnie Ledbetter.

Jerry Bailey's Inside Track, DVD (two volumes). Four hours of horse racing inside information in Q & A format with host Morty Mittenthal and former jockey and Racing Hall of Fame member Bailey. Features Bailey's insightful analysis of jockeys, trainers, horses, horse racing, and handicapping.

Let It Ride, Movie. A very funny movie that used horse racing as it's backdrop. Featured stars Richard Dreyfuss and Teri Garr.

Seabiscuit, Movie. A very good movie about the great race horse, Seabiscuit.

Secretariat, Movie. A movie about Secretariat that also, rather nicely, wove in the story of Secretariat's owner, Penny Chenery Tweedy.

Books about the Kentucky Derby

Run for the Roses: 100 Years at the Kentucky Derby by Jim Bolus. New York: Hawthorn Books, 1974.

Books about Horse Racing and/or the History Of

Legacies of the Turf (Vols. I & II) by Edward L. Bowen. Lexington, KY.: Eclipse Press, 2003, 2004. Biographies of the major Thoroughbred breeders.

Horse Racing's Top 100 Moments by the staff and correspondents of *The Blood-Horse*. Lexington, KY: Eclipse Press, 2006.

Annuals

American Racing Manual. Chicago: Daily Racing Form Publishing Co., 1906 –present. This is an annual recap of everything noteworthy that happened in horse racing that year. In it you'll find all of the graded stakes winners, Eclipse Award winners, top jockeys, top trainers, top owners, and top breeders. Billed as *The Official Encyclopedia of Thoroughbred Racing*, it is likely more than you ever needed or wanted to know. Used primarily as a reference guide. Not good reading material.

Horse Racing Periodicals and Websites

The Blood-Horse. Weekly and online at: www.bloodhorse.com

Thoroughbred Times. Weekly and online at: www.thoroughbredtimes.com

Thoroughbred Daily News. Daily. Website: www.thoroughbreddailynews.com

Daily Racing Form. Daily. Website: www.drf.com

FOOTNOTES

Chapter 2

[1] To learn to read the *Daily Racing Form* go to "http://www.drf.com" and run your cursor over "Tools" on the menu bar of the home page. In the drop-down box you'll see "Fan Education." Run your cursor over that. You'll now see another drop-down menu that offers "Learn to Read the DRF" and "Learn to Play the Races." This is a good place to start your education.

[2] The past performances are just that: a record of each horse's prior races and performance in these races.

Chapter 4

[1] "Pace" refers to the speed of the race as dictated by the front-runners. A solid pace bodes well for a closer and a slow pace helps the front-runners.

Chapter 7

[1] Also referred to as a "blinder," a term I do not care for because it implies the horse is blinded.

[2] "Apprentice year" is the first year a jockey rides. Called apprentice or "bug" riders, they get a five- to 10-pound weight allowance, depending upon how many races they've won.

Chapter 10

[1] *The Encyclopedia of Louisville*, Edited by John E. Kleber, The University of Kentucky Press (c) 2001, pg, 470, column 3

[2] The first Saturday in May is the long standing, traditional date of the Kentucky Derby.

[3] Graded stakes earnings: Graded stakes are the most prestigious stakes races and draw the best horses. Grade I (that's a roman numeral one) is the most formidable; grade II is next; and grade III is the lowest level of graded stakes but still a very tough race as it's still "graded." There are hundreds of stakes races with no grading. To get into the Kentucky Derby a horse must earn enough money in graded stakes.

PHOTO CREDITS

Anne M. Eberhardt photos unless noted.

Suzi Picou Oldham, p. 7; Adam Coglianese, 8; Ken Weaver, 17; Tom Hall, 28; courtesy Donna Barton Brothers, 30, 31, 89; John Korphage, 36; Mathea Kelley, 41; Kinetic, 75; Benoit; Horse Photos/NTRA, 93

Front cover: Anne M. Eberhardt

Back cover: John Korphage